Drug Use and Abuse

JAMES WILLIS

former Consultant Psychiatrist
Guys Hospital and
King's College Hospital, London
and Bexley Hospital, Kent

faber and faber
LONDON · BOSTON

First published in 1989
by Faber and Faber Limited
3 Queen Square London WCIN 3AU

Photoset by Parker Typesetting Service Leicester
Printed in Great Britain by
Richard Clay Ltd, Bungay, Suffolk

© James Willis, 1989

British Library Cataloguing in Publication Data is available

ISBN 0–571–15088–8

For L. J.

Contents

Acknowledgements

First I would like to express my gratitude to the Institute for the Study of Drug Dependence for their permission to reproduce Tables 1–3.

My good friends Dr Cindy Fazey and Dr John Marks both gave me much useful advice and encouragement. My wife, June, typed the draft manuscript and my former secretary Audrey White the final version.

The publishers have been extremely patient with my tardiness and for this I am particularly grateful to Mr Roger Osborne.

Introduction

This book is not intended to be a comprehensive work on the subject of substance abuse. Its brevity and omissions should make that quite obvious. Facts about addictive substances, their effects, hazards and the complications of their use are described for the purpose of information but the intention of the book is to demonstrate that too frequently our ideas concerning drug abuse are influenced by uninformed opinion, myth, bigotry and sheer ignorance – often propagated by the media. Some factual information about substance abuse is given and examples of abuse are described. It is hoped that these may challenge the stereotyped notions too many people have concerning drug usage and drug users.

In this way the book may reflect the fact that the study of substance abuse is both confused and confusing, despite the considerable advances in our understanding of physical, social and psychological aspects of these phenomena.

In no sense is it an attempt to indicate rigid guidelines regarding the management and law enforcement aspects of these problems. It is hoped that it will be regarded as a plea for a sensible, rational and humane attitude towards drug usage.

1

Cultural and Historical Aspects

This is not a comprehensive overview of the history of drug taking. The chapter contains some historical examples of substance abuse which in their cultural context may serve to challenge some of the assumptions we usually make about drugs and drug users. It is not my intention to draw rigid and definitive conclusions from these examples, but to indicate that things are not so simple as they often appear.

It is impossible to study drug abuse in a socio-cultural vacuum. It is not just a matter of looking at the equation drug + person = addiction, and proceeding no further. Drug usage is influenced, modified, even determined by the culture in which a person lives. Cultural influences surrounding a person can control drug-using habits in beneficial ways. The best-known example of this is in the field of alcohol abuse where it is known that some people do not develop problem drinking to any significant degree. For example, Jewish people learn a respect for alcohol from an early age and are educated to its use in the setting of religious observance. It is incorporated into their lives in a way which encourages temperance. This is found too amongst the Lebanese, who treat alcohol with respect and who deride drunkenness. In Italy alcohol problems are less common than in France. Italy has a much lower rate of alcoholism. The reason for this is that drunkenness is regarded unfavourably and alcohol is linked to meals, whereas in France people drink at any time of the night or day. Anyone travelling through northern France and stopping at a café in the early hours for an invigorating cup of coffee will find farm labourers cheerfully consuming cognac and coffee on their way to work, and at lunch-time drinking fortified wines before going home to lunch.

In Islamic countries prohibition of alcohol is relatively effective although many Islamic countries under the influence of Western behaviour have developed a significant population of problem drinkers.

Of course even in societies where alcohol abuse is relatively widespread, most people are able to use alcohol without becoming problem drinkers.

Opium Use in China

A good starting point in the examination of selected cultural examples of drug use is the history of the use of opium in China. Tradition suggests that opium has historically been widely used in China but this is not true. Severe problems of opium use were not apparent until the seventeenth century although usage had begun before then. Instances of opiate use as a self-intoxicant and in medical practice are found in Egyptian, Greek and Roman writings. The history of the use of opium is the history of medicine. The ancient Romans recognized the hazards of chronic opium taking and also the withdrawal symptoms. For many centuries, however, opium use was mainly restricted to the Middle and Near East and hardly reached Europe. Opium is said to have been brought to India by Arab merchants; by the sixteenth century European visitors recognized the production and consumption of opium in the sub-continent.

From the time of the Mogul Empire until the mid-nineteenth century opium production was handled by the Muslim population. This was long after India had been incorporated into the British Empire. Though opium went into China in the seventeenth century, it was still mainly produced in India. In the succeeding centuries the opium habit spread and by the seventeenth century it was so widespread in China that the rulers wanted to stop it. As the opium was imported from India it was a large source of revenue for imperialist Britain, who not only encouraged its growth and trade but, when the Chinese tried to suppress it, fought a series of opium wars with China. The object of the wars was to force the Chinese into continuing to import opium which they didn't want. British military strength was successful and the opium trade was reimposed on the Chinese.

It is likely that opium smoking followed tobacco smoking and it is said to have been brought to China from the Dutch East Indies. However, it spread in China where there was no doubt that a vast number of people were in a state of inertia and apathy due to excessive opium use.

The first attempts to control the opium trade did not begin until 1912 when the International Opium Convention was signed, but there was no evidence that the opium consumption in China fell thereafter. When the Japanese invaded China they encouraged opium taking as a way of buying the co-operation and submissiveness of their victims. So the spread of opium taking in China started with commercial exploitation and continued as a tool for the subjugation of a vanquished enemy. It is said that opium use in China has now been eliminated as a social problem, though like many aspects of life in that distant land this is difficult to prove.

Central Stimulant Abuse in Sweden

Sweden is a country with a long history of a high level of social stability. Freedom from war and economic distress and the development of moderate, progressive social reform have put it high on the list of countries where most people enjoy a good standard of living (also extremely high taxation) and relative freedom from the pressures of unemployment and poverty. Almost a model welfare state.

Sweden has a tradition of maintaining careful records of the incidence and prevalence of illness. The population is relatively static so that Swedish health statistics are accurate and reliable. On the surface it seemed there had never been a problem of widespread drug misuse until the decade from 1957 to 1967 when central stimulant abuse became a major problem. The rarity of drug abuse was an accepted fact. In the early 1930s a small number of people

3

were sleeping-pill abusers but even in the early 1940s a nationwide survey revealed less than a hundred known cases of drug misuse, mainly people taking opiates.

In the late 1930s amphetamines were available in Sweden and people found that they acted as a stimulant and reduced appetite. People valued increased energy plus the ability to work harder and began to value the mythical idea that amphetamines increase sexual potency (in fact they don't).

Central stimulants were advertised in the newspapers and on the radio where they were recommended as a universal remedy for those people who felt weary. The slogan was 'Two pills are better than a month's vacation'. The tablets could be bought across the counter until 1939, when it was apparent that the number of amphetamines consumed annually was increasing. They were then made available only on medical prescription and there was a short-lived reduction in national amphetamine consumption.

In the early 1940s amphetamine taking was widespread but cases of gross abuse and chronic dependency were rare. By 1943 doctors were warned of the growth of amphetamine consumption and this led to amphetamine prescribing being reduced by about 50 per cent. In 1944 amphetamines were placed on the Swedish National Narcotics Drug List and became subject to the same restrictions as narcotic drugs. Medical and public awareness had hardened.

The extent of the problem may be gleaned from the fact that 400,000 tablets were sold in 1938, but by 1942 the total rose to six million. The biggest sales were in cities, where the problems of amphetamine abuse centred.

It was estimated that in the years 1942–3 there were over 200,000 regular amphetamine takers in Sweden, i.e. 3 per cent of the adult population. Of these probably 140,000 were occasional users of whom half took tablets once a year, the other half between two and four times a year. Of the remainder it was said that 60,000 people were taking them twice a month and 4,000 once a week, leaving about 3,000 taking them almost daily in doses of up to ten tablets a day; the dosage of other users being of the order of no more than three or four tablets a day. The number of excessive users was small, probably around two hundred people taking between ten and a hundred tablets a day. This level persisted throughout the 1940s; taking the pills was common, severe abuse was relatively uncommon and accounted for about 0.1 per cent of the total number of amphetamine takers.

From the mid-1950s the picture changed; levels began to increase in 1956 and peaked in 1959. The change was clear not only in numbers but also in the nature of the drug problem. Until the mid-1950s amphetamine taking, though widespread, was almost entirely confined to prescribed medication legally obtained.

But in the 1950s a different type of amphetamine taker emerged:[1] delinquent youngsters with a history of previous criminal behaviour, who fastened on to amphetamines as valued illicitly obtained stimulants. There was an expansion of self-injection. The range of amphetamines used was extensive, involving those previously prescribed by doctors as stimulants and appetite suppressants. By the late 1950s the problem in Sweden reached epidemic proportions – an epidemic ultimately brought under control by a mixture of legal and social measures. It is interesting to speculate why these drugs should have become the chosen drugs in Sweden at that time. During the same period the drug problem in the United Kingdom involved narcotics. For this there is no simple explanation. Stimulant abuse in Japan following the Second World War was something that occurred against a background of a changing society which had undergone severe defeat in war and where morale was low. But in Sweden none of these forces was at work. Here was a peaceful, progressive, stable nation with a law-abiding populace that became involved in an epidemic of delinquent drug abuse. But in the case of both Sweden and Japan, the lesson is much the same, and applies equally to the United Kingdom and the USA – namely that illicit drug use is mainly an activity involving young males who take the drugs for hedonistic reasons. These may have their roots in the quest for euphoria, the need to alleviate painful feelings of one sort or another, or may be part of a picture of

1. For much of the discussion of the Swedish problem and for the statistics cited, see L. Goldberg (1968) 'Drug abuse in Sweden', *Bulletin of Narcotics*, Vol. 20, no 1, p. 1, and Vol. 20, no 2, p. 9.

general isolation and hopelessness in a deprived society. There is a specious quality to many of these simplistic explanations, however, since not every member of the population of, say, Liverpool is a drug user.

When drug misuse reaches epidemic proportions a similar pattern of events recurs. The drug has generally been taken by the higher social classes and spreads downwards to the rest of the population. The social problem arises only when the drug is taken up and misused by people who behave in an anti-social way because this brings their drug habits to the attention of the public. The public, quite naturally, are inclined to blame the drug itself rather than anything else since the supposed 'special' effects of the drug are the most tangible and obvious aspects of the problem. It is often convenient for society to explain away anti-social behaviour by blaming it entirely on drugs but this is frequently a superficial and inadequate explanation. The effects of mind-altering drugs are never predictable; one has to look beyond the drug to gain some understanding. The fundamental question centres upon exactly what society regards as anti-social as opposed to acceptable behaviour, and the significance of this problem is not necessarily related to numbers.

In the USA where drug use is extremely widespread, yet far less common than alcohol abuse, it might be argued that drug abuse receives special attention because it involves mainly the young and is associated with much illness and death. But this is not an adequate explanation since young people engage in all sorts of activities which carry high accident and death rates, such as riding motorcycles. Public concern possibly stems from a puritanical attitude towards the pursuit of pleasure; on the other hand, smoking and overeating don't attract the same attention, though the link between these acts and physical illness is obvious. There is no complete answer to this question.

Some Historical Aspects of Cannabis Use

In 1378 the Emir Soudoun Sheikhounei tried to stop poor people abusing cannabis by having the plants destroyed and the eaters imprisoned; it was also decreed that people so convicted should have their teeth removed. Nevertheless the use of cannabis increased. Cannabis is of particular interest because it is the most widely used illicit drug. It is taken by millions of people all over the world and is said to have the most lengthy history of abuse, having the advantage of growing wild and being relatively cheap. In 2000 BC it was regarded as a sacred grass and from the fifteenth to the seventeenth century Indian physicians regarded it as useful in the treatment of leprosy. Its use probably started in India and then spread to Arabia and other parts of the world.

In ancient Hindu medicine it was used as a sedative, to reduce appetite and to relieve constipation. It was also used for many disorders, ranging from asthma to rheumatic pains. In the Middle East, Asia Minor, Central Asia and India its use is most prevalent among poorer members of the population, particularly in Africa, regardless of whether it is prohibited or not.

In Europe and the USA its use is relatively recent. People started smoking marijuana in Paris around the middle of the nineteenth century, being introduced to it by intellectuals such as Baudelaire and Gautier. At that time the intellectuals and artists who used it would meet together to enjoy its effects, which they then discussed at considerable length. On the whole cannabis use was regarded unfavourably in Europe until quite recently; only since the 1960s has there been a dramatic increase in cannabis use in the Western world. The arguments about its dangers and the question of its illegal status continue. At the same time one has to ask whether society needs yet another intoxicant.

Central Stimulant Abuse: an Epidemic

Between 1945 and 1955 there was in Japan an epidemic of drug abuse which was unique and which was a forerunner of similar problems in Sweden and the United Kingdom. In the past Japan had had a few problems with drug abuse, involving methylamphetamine – the most dangerous of all the amphetamines. But this epidemic began at the end of the Second World War. During the war this drug had been issued free to Japanese troops to improve their energy and

7

increase their fighting spirit. When the war ended it was available over the counter at a time of intense social disorder. It so happened that at that time many drugs were available and the laws on drug control were loosely applied. The rapid spread of methylamphetamine taking could easily be compared to the epidemic spread of an infectious disease.

The first cases were seen in 1945 mainly in cities such as Tokyo and Osaka. Thereafter they spread to smaller towns and to rural areas. The most easily available form of the drug was injectable methylamphetamine, which could be legally obtained. By 1948 a measure of control had been achieved by putting methylamphetamine on the dangerous drug list. Later, further laws were passed to discourage the use of central stimulant drugs.

Despite these measures, by 1954 over two million people were methylamphetamine users and probably around half a million were regular users. The problem started among the upper social classes and then spread downwards throughout society. In poor areas methylamphetamine taking was responsible for delinquency and social disorder. The main group involved was male and aged between nineteen and twenty-five. This chronic amphetamine abuse led to the usual consequences, namely mental disorder (psychosis) caused by drug taking and criminality associated with drug seeking.

The spread of amphetamine taking in Japan was compared with the spread of an infectious disease. It fulfilled all the necessary criteria. It started in a population previously unexposed to drugs and spread with the same speed and virulence as did, for instance, measles in the South Pacific islands – an area where measles had never been found until it was brought there by foreign travellers, causing widespread illness and death.[1]

1. For a fuller description of the Japanese 'epidemic', see H. Brill and T. Hirose (1969) 'The rise and fall of a methylamphetamine epidemic; Japan 1945–1955', *Seminars in Psychiatry*, Vol. 1, p. 179.

Chatorpan

It is interesting to find that substances otherwise regarded as being perfectly harmless can, under special circumstances, become involved in what appears to be an addiction and certainly can affect a person's social behaviour. A good example of this is the condition chatorpan, found among the Hindi-speaking people of western Uttar Pradesh in northern India. In this part of India the condition is regarded by the population as an addictive state in which a person eats an excessive quantity of sweets (*mithai*) and various spicy snacks (*chat*). Because of this excessive consumption they are regarded by the local population as anti-social, since their behaviour is said to deteriorate. This deterioration is ascribed to their excessive preference for these foods. Men involved in this are called *chatora* and women *chatori*. It cannot in any sense be regarded as a medical problem but the general population at least feels that the people involved are dependent on these sweets and snacks.

An investigation of the problem carried out in the late 1960s[1] involved interviewing people right across the general population and obtaining their views on this strange phenomenon. It so happens that in that part of India sweet foods play quite a large part in social and religious activities. Sugar cane is a local crop and so sweets are common. They are offered in worship and at religious festivals, and also play an important part in marriage rituals and ceremonies surrounding childbirth and death.

It is not simply that the person concerned eats too many of these sweets and thereby acquires a bad reputation, but rather that this over-indulgence appears to coincide with rather undesirable personality characteristics. The people involved are regarded by society as worthless, immature individuals who are more than likely to be sexually promiscuous, and they are seen as having entered into a process of moral and social deterioration. Interestingly enough the excessive sweet-eater does slip into some of the anti-social habits of the alcoholic or the drug user, i.e. those unable to meet their needs will resort to cheating, stealing and other means of obtaining sweets.

1. V. P. Vatuk and S. J. Vatuk (1967) 'Chatorpan: a culturally defined form of addiction in North India', *International Journal of Addiction* Vol. 2, p. 103.

The population regard them as criminal in behaviour and as incompetent, inert people who make little or no contribution to society at large. The excessive self-gratification rather than the substance itself is condemned, and this excessive self-gratification is supposed to lead to personal, moral and social decline.

Taking the Powders in Sweden

Phenacetin is a pain-killing drug which has a mildly stimulant effect. It was used in medical practice for many years, usually in combination with aspirin as an over-the-counter remedy. Unfortunately, prolonged phenacetin taking, especially where the normal dose is exceeded, can cause kidney damage leading in certain cases to kidney failure and death.

An intriguing series of events was revealed during the investigation of kidney damage caused by phenacetin taking in the town of Huskvarna in Sweden.[1] The town's main industry is a large factory which produces a wide range of products. At the time of the investigation it had three thousand employees and the investigation concerned was looking for the reasons for the very high prevalence of phenacetin taking in the town. This practice had produced a high death rate from kidney failure.

It all started after the First World War during the pandemic 'Spanish' influenza. One of the local doctors used to prescribe a powder containing caffeine, phenacetin and phenazone. The powder was effective in relieving the severe muscular pains that were a feature of that illness. However, many people who took the powder found that they had renewed energy due to its mild stimulant effect. Like the coca chewers of South America the workers assumed that the stimulant effect might be useful in the factory and the idea spread that this would enable them to work more and earn more. It was not long before these powders were being taken regularly throughout the town. They could be obtained over the counter, and in time regular powder taking became a local custom and a social

1. K. Grimlund (1963) 'Phenacetin and renal damage at a Swedish factory', *Acta Medica Scandinavia*, supplement 405, p. 1.

habit. Powders were handed around rather like cigarettes. Patients in hospital, for instance, would often receive them as gifts from visitors. It became the custom to present brightly coloured packets of the powder to people on their birthdays. The consequence was that in the town the death rate from severe kidney damage was six times as high as that of a larger town near by. In looking for the extent of the powder taking the employees of the factory and members of the population were given questionnaires to complete about their powder-taking habits. The most common reason for taking the powder was given as 'pain', and the most common reason for continuing was 'to maintain high output in the factory'.

The ironic thing was that the people were in no sense addicted to these powders; when the dangers were demonstrated most people stopped. This is cited as an almost classic example of drug abuse – involving a drug which had medical uses being taken excessively and for a long time and for reasons which were quite inconsistent with ordinary medical practice. It was also a good example of the way in which drugs can quickly acquire a spurious reputation and be adopted by a community as an acceptable practice. However, in this case the results were tragic for many people.

A Historical View of Drug Abuse in Britain

Severe problems of narcotic addiction in Britain began in the early 1960s, when a number of people – doctors, members of the Dangerous Drugs Department of the Home Office and others – became aware of an increase in addiction to narcotics. Hitherto the United Kingdom had been regarded by countries with a big drugs problem such as the USA as being fortunate in having an insignificant drug problem.

Self-injection with morphine enjoyed a vogue at the end of the nineteenth century, as did the use of cocaine, but this was confined to small numbers of upper-class people and was not an important problem. It was more of a medico-social curiosity. The proper legal control of narcotic drugs started in 1912, bringing the United Kingdom into line with other countries in the world who had agreed on international and domestic controls. Before 1912 opiates were freely available without prescription. After legal controls were introduced the Home Office monitored the numbers of narcotics addicts. All those receiving prescriptions for narcotics, whether to manage their addiction or for other medical reasons, had their prescriptions recorded in lists kept in retail pharmacies. The inspectors of the Home Office Dangerous Drugs Department inspected these lists regularly and identified the numbers and population.

In the early 1920s a handful of people were receiving regular prescriptions for morphine for the management of their addiction. There was some concern about whether this was the correct thing to do, and in 1926 a parliamentary committee (the Rolleston Committee) reported on the practice. The Committee's main finding was that prescribing opiates on a maintenance basis was a perfectly humane and reasonable thing to do in the face of repeated treatment failures and the inability of the patient to stop being an addict. This practice came to be known as the 'British System' and with hindsight was probably the subject of a good deal of myth. Perhaps the most misleading myth was that the existence of the 'British System' prevented the spread of opiate addiction throughout the population. On the other hand it should be said that the attitude of medical and other people involved was humane and sensible in that narcotics addiction was seen as a medico-social problem and not as a legal and criminal one. The tendency was generally to decriminalize the practice as much as possible, in sharp contrast to the USA where doctors were actively discouraged from treating addicts, and were persecuted if they did. It is not surprising that they gave up. This attitude spilled over into the management of chronic pain. Patients needing adequate pain relief, using narcotics, were unable to get them. This attitude persists in the USA. Happily this was not the case in Britain, though present news is not so good. In any case, the numbers of addicts remained stable, scattered all over the country, mainly middle aged and in no sense members of a drug-using sub-culture. Many were 'therapeutic addicts', also doctors and nurses. Their problem was their own problem; they didn't gather in groups to take drugs. Possibly society might have become complacent about them.

The picture began to change just after the Second World War. The first change was a rise in the number of cannabis offences, at first mainly confined to immigrant West Indians who had brought their cannabis use with them and for whom it was a normal activity. There was also some cannabis use by professional jazz musicians who had picked up the habit in the USA.

In 1951 a significant event occurred – a break-in to a hospital pharmacy. Large quantities of narcotics were stolen and were found being peddled in the streets of London's West End. Not long after this the man involved was arrested and was found to have been a former employee of the hospital. His arrest and the identification of his customers revealed fourteen people who were taking heroin and morphine but who had never been known to official agencies. After the man was imprisoned a total of sixty-three people were identified who had direct or indirect contacts with him. In 1960 the Home Office Dangerous Drugs Department first identified a heroin addict who was below the age of twenty, and thereafter the numbers of notified heroin addicts rose steadily. In 1958 there were a mere four hundred or so, in 1969 nearly three thousand were notified. The street narcotics addicts of the 1960s were youngsters who tended to congregate together, had usually drifted away from home and found some accommodation in central London. They mostly conformed to the stereotype of the typical 'junkie'. It was comparatively easy to obtain heroin on prescription from some doctors, and official concern about this was such that the regulations regarding the prescribing of heroin and cocaine to addicts were changed so that only specially licensed doctors could do this. These were all psychiatrists working in drug dependency clinics in London and later in other cities. The numbers of notified addicts rose steadily and although it appeared in the mid-1970s that they had reached a plateau, there was a steep rise from 1976/77 onwards and in 1985 there were 14,000 new notifications to the Home Office.

It is generally agreed that the notification numbers are an understatement. The official numbers probably represent about a fifth of the real number of addicts so that at the present time there must be at least 50,000 heroin addicts in the United Kingdom. However, this should be seen in the context of the fact that there are at least half a million people in the United Kingdom who have severe alcohol problems, and that abuse of sleeping pills and tranquillizers is widespread. Public attention is too easily focused on heroin, less easily on alcohol, smoking and tranquillizers.

2

What Is Drug Abuse?

How Did We Get Where We Are?

The abuse of drugs is a topic which is difficult to describe factually
since it is riddled with mythology. Many questions remain
unanswered. It is hard to measure the subjective experience a
person undergoes when a mind-altering drug is taken. People who
take these drugs, though they may do so for a variety of personal
and social reasons, do so because they seek the particular subjective
experience that the drug produces within them. Whether this be an
alteration in feeling such as mood elevation and stimulation of
mental and physical activity, whether it be to place a barrier between
the self and the problems of everyday living, or whether for the
purpose of causing changes in perception, the end point is the
same.

As these experiences cannot be measured, we have to rely on
self-report – in itself unreliable. A person's subjective experience of
drug effect is influenced by expectation and may be filtered by
personality factors. On top of this comes information from other
drug users, helping to create a mythology of drug-induced experience. Before we start asking simple questions about all this we are
up against an area where data about subjective drug effects is hard
to come by.

Why do people take drugs? The first thing that should be realized
is that the act of taking a drug does not imply a state of dependence
or addiction. We might equally well inquire why it is that the

majority of people experimenting with drugs do not become dependent upon them, in the same way that the majority of people who experiment with the most commonly used drug – alcohol – do not develop alcohol-related problems.

The Definition of Drug Dependence

Drug dependence is not easy to define. The American Psychiatric Association in its *Diagnostic and Statistical Manual* (DSM 3) produced a set of diagnostic criteria which could be applied to 'abuse' and dependence. It has now been suggested that the category called 'abuse' should be taken out and that dependence could be defined as a syndrome of significant behaviour that indicates a serious degree of involvement with a mind-altering drug. In this case persons who meet three or more of the following criteria would receive a diagnosis of dependence.

1 The repeated effort to cut down or control substance abuse.
2 Frequent intoxication or impairment by substance abuse when the person is expected to fulfil social or occupational obligations (absenteeism, attending work while 'high', driving when drunk).
3 The need for increased amounts of the substance to create intoxication or the desired effect, or experiencing less effect whilst using the same amount of the substance (tolerance).
4 Withdrawal symptoms.
5 Preoccupation with looking for or taking the substance.
6 Giving up important social, job-related or recreational activities in order to look for or take the substance.
7 Frequent use of the substance to avoid withdrawal symptoms.
8 More frequent use of the substance in larger doses or over a longer period than was intended.
9 Continued substance use despite physical or mental illness or despite a particular social problem that the person well knows is made worse by use of the substance.
10 The presence of mental or physical illness that is an established complication of prolonged substance usage.

Though addiction is a term which has been long and perhaps too much used, and the term dependence is no doubt preferable, the word 'addiction' immediately conjures up the way in which a person becomes totally involved with drug use and loses control.

What is addiction?

The term 'addiction' has never been easy to define and is frequently avoided but like other words used by doctors it is likely to outlive its obituarists. It has at least the merit of being short. Nowadays the term 'dependence' is preferred. This is defined as a state in which a person has a compulsion to take drugs for hedonic reasons and also to avoid withdrawal symptoms if drug use is stopped. Dependence can be physical where there is a clear interaction between the drug and cells in the central nervous system producing a physical need to take the drug.

There is always psychological dependence, i.e. the emotional drive to continue, usually associated with craving. Possibly in the past undue emphasis has been placed on differentiating between these varieties of dependence.

The term 'tolerance' refers to a drug-related effect in which a person needs increasing doses to achieve the desired effect or to prevent withdrawal symptoms. This is a purely physiochemical effect.

Dependence then is the preferred term in a scientific sense but in this book the word 'addict' or 'addiction' will be used as synonyms.

An Introduction to Drug Abuse

Drug abuse causes much concern, national and international. From time to time society panics about drug misuse and one can scarcely open a newspaper without seeing a reference to it. The panic then subsides and the topic disappears from the media; and one is spared the sight of one's colleagues appearing on television, looking uncomfortable and making the same comments over and over again.

Human beings have intoxicated themselves for pleasure and for relief from distress for many hundreds, even thousands of years.

The history of opium and cannabis indicates this clearly. Self-intoxication probably pre-dates farming, since Stone Age caves have revealed evidence of poppy heads which had been heated and the fumes inhaled. Perhaps Stone Age people had better reasons to indulge in self-intoxication than we do. In the main, however, the past three hundred years have seen the expansion of widespread alcohol and drug abuse, particularly during the last hundred years and ultimately on the largest scale since the Second World War, affecting nearly every country in the world.

Large-scale substance abuse is not so much a new problem, rather one which has intensified as technology has improved. A wider range of drugs has emerged and methods of delivering larger doses are available. It should be realized, too, that despite legal, social and cultural restraints that are placed on people's behaviour, if an individual wants to intoxicate himself or herself, either occasionally or continually, he or she will do so. This may be because the person wants to get 'high' or it may be used as a remedy against misery and hopelessness; it may also be influenced by fashion. History provides many examples of this last instance.

Another factor is the fluctuation in availability of a particular intoxicant. For example, when the prohibition of alcohol was introduced in the USA there was a significant switch from alcohol consumption to the use of drugs such as morphine and cocaine. However, in a short space of time the amount of alcohol consumed was greater than it had been before prohibition and indeed by the time prohibition was repealed this was certainly the case. In the first two years of prohibition the admissions to hospital for alcoholism decreased significantly but within three years they had risen to the pre-prohibition figure.

Another good example of this phenomenon occurred in Ulster in the mid-nineteenth century, when people switched their allegiance from alcohol to ether.

Alcohol abuse in Irish people and Irish expatriates is well documented. In the mid-nineteenth century there was a considerable amount of illicit spirit distilling all over Ireland. However, this diminished as a result of a number of factors. First of all there was failure of the corn crops, second the police were more zealous in seeking out illicit distilleries and, third, Ireland was still recovering from a temperance campaign preached by the famous Father Mathew which had caused half a million Irishmen to take the pledge!

It so happened that at the time when consumption of illicitly distilled alcohol decreased in Ulster, a fair amount of ether was used for medicinal purposes. This was widely available due to a recent cholera epidemic, the medical profession having the mistaken notion that ether was useful in the treatment of cholera. People soon found that by drinking ether they could become intoxicated very rapidly, and recover just as quickly. In the area of Ulster centring around Cookstown – an area about a thousand square miles in size – it was reckoned that 50,000 people across all social classes were regular ether drinkers, and the annual consumption was about 17,000 gallons. The ether was imported from the United Kingdom and on market days the streets reeked of it and people were seen to be staggering around under its influence. The effect of the ether is quick so that the drinker goes from drunkenness to sobriety and back to drunkenness in a matter of hours. Happily, only a small amount is actually absorbed since it vaporizes very quickly in the stomach causing belching and nausea. Hardened ether drinkers learned to slow this process down by drinking ice-cold water beforehand so as to stop the ether vaporizing! Despite widespread public concern, sermons preached in the pulpit, articles in the lay and medical press, it appears that on the whole people didn't come to too much harm through drinking ether and the epidemic subsided fairly quickly when grain became more available and people were able to return to home distilling.

This switch from one sort of intoxicant to another is very common when supplies run low. The heroin addict will resort to sleeping pills, tranquillizers and stimulant pills if supplies of heroin run out. In the same way, people with severe alcohol habits may become dependent on heavy doses of sleeping tablets and tranquillizers. There are telling examples of the fact that once dependency is established the drive to go on on taking a particular drug is very strong. One has only to think of the anguish and distress exhibited by many heavy smokers when they are politely requested not to smoke.

What Is a Drug?

It is important to define the term 'drug'. The usual definition is that a drug is any substance that when taken into the living organism may modify one or more of that organism's functions. This definition covers a diverse range of naturally occurring and synthetic substances which have a wide range of medical usage. It involves substances ranging from simple, pain-relieving drugs such as aspirin to the increasingly sophisticated medications used in the treatment of infections, metabolic disorders, cancer and many illnesses which until recently were virtually untreatable. This last must be emphasized: until the Second World War, doctors had access to a limited number of medications. The only drugs available for the treatment of infections were the sulfonamides, until the break-through in the Second World War when penicillin was first used in the treatment of hitherto untreatable infections. The explosion in the development of antibiotics is remarkable. A dictionary of antibiotics is a substantial tome listing names and uses of several hundred compounds and all this has come about in a relatively short time. This is particularly so in the case of drugs used in the treatment of cancer, where it seems as though a new one appears almost every week. Doctors can now call upon an array of potent medications. Most doctors are familiar with only a limited range of medications since it would be impossible to know about all of them. Thus a psychiatrist will use mind-altering (psychoactive) drugs, the cardiologists will use drugs that act on the heart and the blood pressure, and when the psychiatrist needs advice about the treatment of high blood pressure, if sensible he or she will not prescribe the medication but take advice from a specialist in internal medicine.

At the same time the public have become aware of the medical and allied uses of mind-altering drugs such as the tranquillizers since these are freely prescribed and consumed. Like it or not, we live in a pill-orientated age and this need to take mind-altering drugs in treatment is something that has only recently come under scrutiny. Any consideration of the problems of drug abuse has to be seen against this background of drug use along conventional medical lines. Drugs that are abused are psychoactive drugs, that is to say they

alter the mental state and function. These alterations can be sedative, i.e. depressing brain function, producing calmness and sleep,
and if excessive coma and death. Or they may be stimulants,
producing alertness and hilarity. There are also drugs which cause
bizarre effects on the mental state so that a person becomes mud-
dled in thinking, may develop hallucinations in which he or she
either sees visions or hears voices or may develop other disturbances of perception in which the environment is perceived in a
distorted way. Indeed the disturbance may be so great that the drug
may induce delusions. These can be thought of as ideas which are
blatantly untrue but which are held with firm conviction in the face
of all logical argument and are a direct result of taking the drug.

The Natural History of Drug Abuse

Addiction is not a static condition. It is a mistake to believe that
people take drugs, become addicted and remain so for ever. This is
an over-simplistic view of the problem and there is now a better
understanding of the history of drug addiction as a process which
may follow a variety of courses.

First, there is experimental drug use where someone takes a drug
probably out of curiosity and often under the influence of friends
who are experimenting with the drug. Many people stop taking
drugs after a period of experimentation and it is likely that this is the
most common form of drug use. Some authorities have claimed that
more than 90 per cent of experimental drug users discontinue after
a few tries.

The next stage is recreational use, where drugs are taken regularly but at intervals, e.g. at weekends. Somehow the use is kept
under control and a pattern of long-term dependence is not
developed. This concept was regarded with caution until comparatively recently when pockets of intermittent drug users came to
light. The author's experience has confirmed this when learning
about a group of people who had been regularly injecting themselves with illicitly obtained heroin at weekends over a period of
years. They had not developed long-term dependence. They lived
normal lives during the working week and took heroin only at the

weekend. Heroin is a highly dependence-producing drug and a course of action such as this is obviously not recommended but it serves to illustrate that addiction is not necessarily manifested as a continual craving. It is certainly the case that intermittent use can apply to alcohol since the vast majority of people who drink alcohol do not become dependent on it and may take it quite infrequently. This is in the face of the fact that alcohol is one of the most damaging of all drugs because of the widespread nature of its use, and because of its real direct physical and psychological dangers.

Finally, there is dependent use when drugs or alcohol are taken frequently throughout twenty-four hours purely to avoid or relieve withdrawal distress. Another aspect of dependent drug use is craving, in which a person has an intense desire to get hold of the drug either to experience its pleasurable effects or to abolish withdrawal symptoms or both. This drug-seeking drive can be very powerful. Someone in need of the next dose of heroin who is unable to obtain it will certainly go to great lengths to do so. A twenty-seven-year-old heroin addict came to a clinic asking for help. He wanted prescriptions for injectable heroin. Three fingers had been amputated from his left hand three weeks previously following the accidental self-injection of crushed sleeping tablets into an artery. Despite all this he still wanted to inject into veins in the infected amputation stump! And people ask 'Why can't addicts stop taking drugs?' The simple fact that people are prepared to spend up to £100 or more a day on illicitly obtained drugs indicates the strength of the drive to continue, despite the fact that the user is well aware of the possible dangers.

No doubt the same drive was true of people in the time of prohibition in the USA. It was certainly true in the author's experience when working in the Middle East in countries where alcohol was totally forbidden. Westerners would go to extravagant lengths to obtain illicitly distilled alcohol – a highly dangerous thing to do – or else spend wildly ridiculous amounts of money on imported bootleg liquor. This provided an interesting example of behaviour among a normal population of expatriates who, to obtain their usual beverages, behaved in the same way that addicts do, i.e. breaking the law every day. And these otherwise respectable people did so without a moment's hesitation. It was a normal part of life. No doubt such people would be the first to condemn the delinquent behaviour of addicts in their own home countries who break the law in order to obtain the drug they want. And it should be noted that these expatriates were not alcohol dependent – they wanted to enjoy the pleasures of social drinking!

The use of psychoactive drugs is firmly established in medical practice. The mind-altering drugs used in practice include the narcotics used for pain relief, and also newer psychoactive drugs which first came into use in the 1950s with the advent of neuroleptics used in the treatment of major mental disorders. However, the most widely used psychoactive drugs are the tranquillizers which were given to patients with symptoms of stress and anxiety.

The final group of psychoactive drugs with respectable medical uses include the anti-depressants included in the treatment of depressive disorders. These came on the market in the mid-1950s and are now prescribed widely – possibly too widely. The most commonly used addictive drugs include:

1 tobacco;
2 alcohol;
3 narcotics (opioids and allied drugs);
4 sedatives – these depress mental activity and include barbiturate and non-barbiturate sleeping tablets; the tranquilllizers are also included in this group since their abuse potential is now recognized;
5 central stimulant drugs which accelerate mental activity – these include cocaine and the amphetamines and related drugs;
6 psychedelics, e.g. LSD, psilocybin, cannabis etc;
7 volatile solvents taken by inhalation, including various glues and dry-cleaning fluids.

These substances will be considered in more detail in further chapters.

Addictive Drugs in Medical Practice

The narcotics which in general are highly addictive induce drowsiness and relieve pain. In the latter function they are of prime importance in medical practice. They include naturally occurring opiates such as morphine extracted from opium, and other commonly used medications such as codeine. Despite the addiction-producing potential of these medications it should be emphasized that narcotic drugs are some of the most important types of drugs that a doctor can prescribe. The relief of pain of whatever degree is a prime duty of the physician. Often all that a doctor can do for a patient is to relieve pain, and the doctor who fails in this duty fails the patient badly. For many years the only drugs that doctors had to offer patients were opiates, and it is unhappily still the case that doctors do not receive proper training in pain relief. It is also lamentable to find the doctor's ability to prescribe for the relief of pain interfered with by ignorant busybodies who have an exaggerated fear that patients may become addicted in the course of the treatment of illnesses such as terminal cancer.

Sedatives used to induce sleep have in the past been prescribed rather irresponsibly by doctors who were often unaware of the long-term hazards of chronic intoxication. Today there is a much greater degree of control over sedative medications and they are less widely used, but there is always need for caution.

Central stimulant drugs are hardly used at all. Again, they will be considered later. Their addiction-producing potential is high and they can cause states of agitation and psychosis. Psychedelic drugs have no medical uses. Alcohol has no medical uses.

Why Do People Take Drugs?

This is the most difficult question of all to answer. People take drugs for many reasons and these involve biological, pharmacological, social and personality-related factors. It is difficult to find one single determinant of drug use for the simple reason that the populations studied have on the whole failed to distinguish between experimental and dependent use, so that our present state of knowledge is confused. Most studies on drug users have been carried out retrospectively, rather like taking a school photograph in year X, looking at it and then making pronouncements about the persons involved. The proper way to look at people who are using drugs is prospectively and prospective studies are thin on the ground.

Alfred R. Lindesmith stated a general addiction theory[1] in which he said that people who use drugs become addicted once they have developed a state of physical dependence so that they use drugs mainly to relieve withdrawal distress. To date this is probably the simplest and best explanation of the dependent process.

Other authors such as Ausubel[2] linked the use of mind-altering drugs in the dependent process as being most likely to develop in people who are immature and who are unable to postpone the gratification of immediate pleasure-seeking.

Others take a different view and relate dependent drug usage to the way in which the user establishes relationships with society in general. In this respect there are probably two theories that are of the most interest. The first is that of Lee N. Robbins[3] who favours the 'natural history' of drug dependence where drug abuse proceeds to dependence and is ultimately determined by time, place, environment and availability. Robbins highlights the way in which those who abuse prescribed drugs contain a strong population of medical and paramedical personnel. Drug abuse in general is regarded by Robbins as a form of socially unacceptable behaviour sometimes related to adolescent rebellion and often related to anti-social personality disorders.

Charles Winick[4] supports a role theory of drug usage in that

1. A. R. Lindesmith (1980) 'A general theory of addiction to opiate type drugs', in *Theories of Drug Abuse*, Research Monograph 30, National Institute on Drug Abuse, pp. 34–7.
2. D. P. Ausubel (1980) 'An interactional approach to addiction', in *Theories on Drug Abuse*, op. cit., pp. 4–7.
3. L. N. Robbins (1980) 'The natural history of drug abuse', in *Theories on Drug Abuse*, op. cit. pp. 215–24.
4. C. Winick (1980) 'A theory of drug dependence, based on role and attitudes towards drugs', in *Theories on Drug Abuse*, op. cit., pp. 225–35.

people who tend to become drug dependent are more likely to have easy access to drugs, total disregard for the forbidden nature of drug usage, and also uncertainty of their social roles.

Chemical theories of the dependent process are best exemplified by those of Vincent Dole and Marie Nyswander,[1] who developed the methadone maintenance programme (see page 95). Their assumption, to date unproven, is that diamorphine dependence is ultimately a metabolic disorder – not a psychological problem. They discount the importance of the reasons for first usage and look for an inherent metabolic disturbance.

Other Theories Regarding the Spread of Drug Abuse

A pill a day keeps the doctor away. We live in a pill-orientated age and people look to psychoactive drugs for the relief of every sort of human discomfort. In this they have been encouraged by doctors and by the drug-manufacturing industry, which has produced psychoactive drugs able to elevate the spirits, relieve tension and help people to feel calm in the face of stress. Unhappily, the price paid for this proliferation of self-medication has been the development of dependence on prescribed psychoactive drugs.

For the dependent user too, symptom relief is an important aspect of the problem. The use of intravenous heroin, barbiturates, cocaine or whatever can place a barrier between the person and his other problems in living. This is something that becomes more prevalent in times of grinding poverty. In Liverpool the average heroin user is likely to be a badly educated, hopeless youngster, usually unemployed and probably unemployable. For such a person heroin provides the sort of relief that gin did in the days of Hogarth.

Genuine curiosity about the effects of drugs is an important factor when looking at the effects of drug use in young people, who are curious about everything. This is one of the great virtues of youth. Whether it be sex, riding motorcycles, scuba diving or drugs,

1. V. P. Dole and M. E. Nyswander (1967) 'Heroin addiction – a metabolic disease', *Archives of Internal Medicine*, Vol. 120, pp. 19–24.

their curiosity is genuine and cannot be overcome simply by point-ing out the dangers. Indeed this may incite even greater curiosity. How forcefully it operates in producing dependent drug use is an open question.

Pressure from other people (peer groups) is an important factor. One has only to look back at one's youth to remember the pressures to take up smoking cigarettes imposed by one's friends who regarded it as a 'manly' thing to do. It is of course a fatally stupid thing to do. Interestingly enough this 'manly' aspect of the smoking problem may be reflected in the women's liberation process. Women now smoke and drink more alcohol than formerly, and this may well be due to their wish to achieve a spurious parity with men.

Looking at larger populations of serious drug users such as narcotics users, the prevailing impression is that the person most at risk from narcotics abuse is a youngster, probably from a poor background, who has a considerably low degree of self-esteem and a poor self-image. Someone who finds it hard to cope with the vagaries of existence whether at school or in an attempt to find a job that can't be found, and who may ultimately be summed up by the rather cruel word – inadequate.

The relationship of criminality to the causes of drug dependence is another matter altogether. Studies in the United Kingdom indicate that the majority of narcotic drug users have a long history of criminal behaviour pre-dating drug use. This is an inescapable finding, but is often incorrectly used to support the idea that all drug abusers and alcoholics are social deviants (see page 28).

The disruptive environment theory

Isadore Chein and his associates[1] looked to the disruptive environ-ment theory as being specifically relevant in the causes of juvenile drug abuse. His studies carried out in the 1960s indicate that a population of narcotics users they were examining had highly specific attitudes towards life and towards drug use which seemed

1. I. Chein, D. L. Gerard, R. S. Lee and E. Rosenfeld (1964) *Narcotics Delinquency and Social Policy – the Road to H,* Tavistock Publications, London; I. Chein (1980) 'Psychological, social and epidemiological factors in juvenile drug use', in *Theories on Drug Abuse,* Research Monograph 30, National Institute on Drug Abuse, pp. 76–82.

to bear a close relationship to their family environment. In the main the population studied were Blacks and Hispanics who came from homes where their parents had no expectations and found it near enough impossible to look after, care for or support their children to any great extent. The children's behaviour was not determined in general by any consistent display of attitudes towards good or bad behaviour. This is in line with most of the studies on juvenile delinquents in the Western world, which indicate quite clearly that where there is no attempt at control, no setting of standards, the children will become delinquents. It has been shown beyond any doubt that this is most applicable to those families which are large and unsupervised.

Denial and Drug Abuse

A striking feature of drug abuse is that in the early stages the user is quite convinced that the habit can be controlled. It is therefore wrong to suppose that people are most amenable to treatment in the early stages. Exactly the reverse is true since the individual concerned is quite convinced that he or she can handle drug taking and that there is no problem. Warnings by teachers, parents, the police, the media etc. are disregarded. Ultimately the drug user has to face the realization that the drug is interfering with his or her life to a substantial degree, and this takes time. Even faced with the physical complications of the abuse of alcohol, the loss of one's job or break-up of a marriage, the user will not accept that the drug is to blame – he or she simply denies the possibility.

Deviant Behaviour and Drug Abuse

There is a theory based on the unverified assumption that drug and alcohol abusers tend to be socially deviant before they develop a dependent substance-abuse status. Such a theory is attractive to those who would regard anyone who is a drug user or problem drinker as being deviant. But really it is a convenient way of using what doctors call the 'dumping syndrome'. In other words, a way of saying 'these people would have developed it anyway so why bother doing anything about it'.

The Pharmacology of Drug Dependence

When discussing drug dependence psychologists stress the psychological aspects, psychiatrists its psychiatric aspects, sociologists its sociological aspects and pharmacologists its pharmacological aspects.

Such is the current climate of thinking about drug-related problems that the pharmacological aspects receive the least consideration. Too often the problems of drug abuse are dismissed with the naïve statement, 'of course it's a social problem'. In this work, written for non-specialist readers, a knowledge of pharmacology is not expected or sought. On the other hand a few basic facts about pharmacology will, it is hoped, be of some use.

How drugs act

Drug activity results from a chemical interaction with a human (or animal) organism. In general there are two ways in which they act. Some act over a large area of the body, as for example drugs which are inhaled, like anaesthetic gases. But the majority of drugs exert a specific action which is directed towards drug receptors: the interfaces between the molecules of the drug and the cells on which they act. Receptors are particular areas of cells in different places in the body. Drugs interact with the receptors and the interaction causes the drug effect. Some have compared the action of drugs upon receptors as a reaction which resembles that of a lock and key.

There are a number of ways in which drugs may act; for instance, they may depress bodily and mental activity. Examples of this include sleeping pills such as the barbiturates, and alcohol. Other drugs can block types of bodily activity: a typical example is the antihistamine drugs, which block allergic reactions. Again, some drugs act as substitutes for normal bodily activity. Examples of this include insulin used in the treatment of insulin-dependent diabetes, and the use of hormones in hormone-replacement therapy. Perhaps the best-known group of drugs are those which destroy invading organisms – the antibiotics.

Other drugs enhance the activity of the brain by stimulation. In the field of drug dependence the two best examples are the amphetamines and cocaine. Finally, perhaps the most homely and most commonly used type of drug activity is that of irritation, e.g. laxatives. Widely consumed, probably too widely, they produce for millions of people every day the homely satisfaction of a well-formed stool.

Certain terms used need to be clarified. Tolerance is a condition where drug effects, desired by the user, can be achieved only by taking high doses. This occurs with pain-killers such as the opiates used in the treatment of terminal illness; also, and more important, in the case of chronic drug abusers who need higher doses to avoid withdrawal distress. Withdrawal symptoms are those physical effects which occur when a drug which induces tolerance and dependence is withdrawn. The most important producers of physical withdrawal symptoms are the opiates, alcohol, barbiturates and benzodiazepines. Withdrawal from alcohol and barbiturates can cause death if withdrawal fits occur and the person chokes on his or her vomit and asphyxiates.

Drug dependence is not properly understood but the available evidence indicates that being addicted has to do with pharmacological changes in the central nervous system. Cells in the system are constantly bombarded with the drug and adapt in a different way so that the person is willing to tolerate what is going on in his or her brain. Repeated drug taking induces these changes. Although we do not presently understand the nature of these changes, or at least only partly understand them, this is the essence of the process. For instance, in opiate dependence a drug such as heroin hits the endogenous receptor, i.e. the opiate receptor within the brain (an enkephalin). This drug activity depresses the production of the endogenous (brain-bound) enkephalin, with the consequence that when the opiate is discontinued the endogenous enkephalin is not sufficient to prevent withdrawal distress.

In the case of dependence on drugs which suppress central nervous activity, e.g. alcohol, barbiturates and benzodiazepine tranquillizers, it seems that these substances alter the activity of another central nervous transmitter in the brain, namely GABA (gamma-aminobutyric acid). The theory is that the actions of GABA are enhanced in a way that is not understood, the end result being that the brain cuts down on the production of GABA. Then if the drugs are withdrawn a rebound effect occurs and withdrawal symptoms develop. In the case of central nervous stimulant drugs such as amphetamines and cocaine, no physical dependence occurs and there are no physical withdrawal symptoms.

Psychological Factors in Drug Dependence

There is much disagreement here. On the one hand are those who believe that dependent drug usage is linked to specific personality-linked factors ('the addiction-prone personality'). Alternatively, there are those who see drug dependence as a process which is determined by psychodynamics, i.e the interplay of conflict, repressed feelings within the person and conflict within the family producing a reaction in the individual which leads the person to become drug dependent.

These arguments have not been resolved. There is evidence that many drug users do so because the drug provides feelings of relief from disturbed mood states (dysphoria) and that there are drug users who cannot cope with painful feelings such as shame, anger, varying states of depression and isolation without resorting to drugs.

Narcotics may help such people to feel better. Unfortunately most of the studies that have been carried out on drug users in this respect have been retrospective and thus are suspect since they look at the person's past history and make deductions from it which may be fallacious. Also, many of the findings in this sort of study apply equally well to groups of individuals with psychiatric problems who are not drug users and who turn out to be remarkably similar in their emotional development and psychopathology.

Finally, it has not been clearly established what may be the long-term effects on an individual's personality anyway. Drugs such as the opiates do interfere with central transmitting substances in the brain and it could well be that repeated drug use could produce permanent personality change. Certainly personality change as

31

observed by parents, friends, etc. while the drugs are being used is definite though temporary. In addition to all this, the need to get hold of the drug by whatever means including theft, and the adoption of a delinquent role can in themselves change a person since he or she is obliged to behave in a persistently deviant way.

3

A Problem for Society

The Dimensions of the Problem

The problems of drug abuse throughout the world have increased greatly in recent times. However, it is not easy to be precise about the numbers involved since past population studies were somewhat unreliable. However, if we take 1977 as a starting point we find an international survey based on information obtained from research workers in twenty-five different countries. The authors reported on the numbers of 'opiate addicts' in the countries concerned and some of the figures included are: the USA 620,000, Iran 400,000, Thailand 350,000, Hong Kong 80,000, Canada 18,000, Singapore 13,000, Australia 12,500, Italy 10,000 and the United Kingdom 6,000.

The numbers have increased substantially since that time and if one takes the reported figures for the United Kingdom in 1988 and multiplies them by four, the generally agreed factor, this gives 50,000 heroin addicts. When one realizes that in the early 1950s in the United Kingdom the number of heroin addicts known to the Home Office was of the order of a few hundred, the escalation of the problem is clear.

The figures for heroin addiction and alcohol are probably the most reliable that we have. Most countries require official listings of heroin addicts based on hospital admissions, criminal offences and, in the United Kingdom, once the diagnosis is made notification to the Home Office Dangerous Drugs Department is mandatory. In the case of all other drugs the figures are much harder to come by. The fact remains that even the official figures always represent an underestimate – on this there is universal agreement. The most unreliable sources come from individuals who are 'experts' in the field and who often make startling pronouncements based on their own personal experience.

Some Attempts at Control

There are two constants in the history of drug use. First, the persistent way in which people choose to intoxicate themselves. Second, the constant attempts by society over the centuries to control this behaviour by means which have been useless and which astonish us by their inappropriate savagery. Some examples of this may give us pause for thought.

The first recorded use of opium goes back to 5000 BC in the Sumerian culture. By 3000 BC alcohol was being made, and by 2500 BC cave dwellers were consuming poppy heads.

In seventeenth century Russia one of the Tsars introduced a law which stated that anyone in possession of tobacco should be tortured until he divulged the name of the dealer. By 1650 tobacco was prohibited in various European countries and in the Ottoman Empire Sultan Murad IV introduced the death penalty for smoking tobacco. 'Even on the battlefield he would surprise men smoking when he would punish them by beheading, hanging, quartering or crushing their hands and feet...' In Germany in 1691 the death penalty was administered in Lüneberg for smoking tobacco. In 1919 the Eighteenth Amendment was added to the US Constitution. It prohibited alcohol and remained in force until 1933 – it had disastrous consequences.

Legal Aspects of Drug Dependence

The development of legislation in Britain surrounding the control of dangerous drugs goes back to 1868, since when a variety of laws, Orders in Council, proclamations, regulations and Acts – over forty in all – have been passed. While it is not possible to review these in detail, the following gives a brief résumé of some of the more relevant.

1 The Pharmacy Act 1868: this was a straightforward attempt to gain some degree of control over opium and opium derivatives.

2 In 1912 the United Kingdom was one of the signatories of the International Opium Convention (Hague Convention). This was the first major concerted effort to establish a degree of control over the production, sale and distribution of opium. The object was to limit opium production to medical purposes only and to list the channels of distribution. Britain, it will be recalled, had a somewhat murky reputation in this respect following the Opium Wars in the nineteenth century, when Britain had virtually reimposed the import of opium into a reluctant China.

3 In 1916 there was concern about soldiers on leave in London who were incorrectly said to obtain cocaine from prostitutes. As a result of co-operation between the police and the military, cocaine and opium were controlled by Defence of the Realm Regulation 40B. The legal control of dangerous drugs remained in a confused state until 1920.

4 The Dangerous Drugs Act 1920: this was a comprehensive law aimed at control of dangerous drugs by regulating their manufacture and prescription, storage and dispensing. Over the years that followed the Act was amended and modified. Originally it controlled opium and opioid drugs. However, with the passage of time new synthetic drugs came under its control: various further pieces of legislation were passed regulating prescriptions etc. In 1923 penalties for infringement of the Act were increased.

5 In 1925 the United Kingdom was one of the signatories of the Geneva Convention. The Dangerous Drugs Act 1925 extended legal control to coca leaves and Indian hemp. The inclusion of Indian hemp as a 'dangerous drug' in the United Kingdom or 'narcotic' in the USA, is clearly relevant to the current controversy over cannabis. It appears that the main pressure for its inclusion came from Egypt and South Africa, two nations where

cannabis taking was widespread. The impression was created that cannabis was as dangerously dependence-producing as the opiates, and this impression was uncritically accepted. The consequence was that cannabis became subject to the same legal sanctions as the opiates. Current thinking suggests that it is less dangerous and should therefore be subject to less punitive sanctions.

6 The Report of the Departmental Committee on Morphine and Heroin Addiction (the Rolleston Report) was published in 1926. The Report reviewed the practice of prescribing narcotics for established addicts and recommended that though in general this could be regarded as reasonable practice it should be restricted to those addicts who had repeatedly failed in treatment.

7 The Drugs (Prevention of Misuse) Act 1964: the Act made it an offence to import or to possess without authority substances listed in the schedule of the Act, including methaqualone.

8 The Dangerous Drugs Act 1965: this Act codified earlier laws and extended control to all the substances listed in the United Nations Single Convention of Narcotic Drugs 1961.

9 The Dangerous Drugs Act 1967 empowered the Home Secretary to regulate the notification of addicts and the prescription of drugs to them. Anyone suspected of being addicted to a drug covered by the Act had to be notified to the chief medical officer of the Home Office Dangerous Drugs Department. The Act also limited the prescription to addicts of heroin and/or cocaine to licensed doctors.

10 The Medicines Act 1968: this Act provided for the control and clinical trial of therapeutic substances and for their development and manufacture under proper supervision.

11 The Misuse of Drugs Act 1971 came into effect on 1 July 1973, superseding the Dangerous Drugs Acts of 1965 and 1967 and the Drugs (Prevention of Misuse) Act 1964. It was a response to the increased problems of drug usage in the United Kingdom. It was intended as a comprehensive piece of legislation to regulate the previous separate legislative items in much the same way, say, as the Mental Health Act 1959 replaced several rather cumbersome pieces of legislation dealing with the mentally ill.

The main provisions of the Act included, first, a power given to the Home Secretary to introduce controls of drugs without having to await recommendations from an international body. Thus he may by Order in Council add new drugs to the schedules of those already controlled. Second, the Act introduced legal procedures to investigate and control irresponsible prescribing. Third, it separated drugs of dependence and misuse into three groups, A, B and C, relative to their harmfulness, and created new offences to check trafficking, increasing the penalties for trafficking and smuggling. It also maintained the power of the police to stop and search those suspected of illicit possession.

12 In addition to the three classes established by the 1971 Act, The Misuse of Drugs Regulations 1986 (which came into effect in April 1986) divided controlled drugs into five schedules, and determined the level of control applied to the drug in question. The drugs in Schedule 1 are the most stringently controlled, and include the active ingredients of cannabis and LSD. There is no way in which these drugs, for instance, can be used medically and they could be supplied for research, for example, only with a licence from the Home Office.

Drugs included under Schedules 2, 3 and 4 comprise the majority of controlled drugs, all of which can be used medically but only upon prescription. It is interesting to note that benzodiazepine tranquillizers are controlled by the Regulations.

The 1986 Regulations determine in detail how the various drugs may be prescribed and administered, and also give detailed instructions to manufacturers, suppliers, doctors and others regarding keeping records and writing prescriptions.

The three classes (A, B and C) of drugs covered by the Misuse of Drugs Act 1971 determine the level of penalties that will be handed out to people who are in illicit possession, trafficking, etc.

Tables 1 and 2 show the main types of controlled drugs by schedule and class, and the penalties for possession and trafficking. Table 3 lists a selection of controlled drugs, again indicating schedule and class.

37

Table 1 Main types of controlled drugs by schedule and class

Schedule	Class under Misuse of Drugs Act		
	A	B*	C
1	Active ingredients of cannabis Hallucinogens Raw opium Coca leaf	Cannabis and cannabis resin	
2	Strong opiates and opioids (heroin, morphine etc.) Cocaine Phencyclidine (PCP)	Strong stimulants (amphetamine, methylphenidate etc.) Weaker opiates and opioids (codeine etc.) Methaqualone and mecloqualone	Dextropropoxyphene
3		Pentazocine Barbiturates	Weaker stimulants (diethylpropion, phentermine etc.) Some sedatives and hypnotics (e.g. meprobamate)
4			Benzodiazepine tranquillizers
5‡	Preparations containing opium, morphine, certain opioids, and cocaine	Non-injectable preparations containing codeine and other weak opiates and opioids	Preparations containing dextropropoxyphene to be taken by mouth

* Any class B drug in injectable form is treated as a class A drug.
‡ Includes dilute and/or small-dose preparations of certain of the drugs listed in Schedule 2.

Table 2 Maximum penalties in the UK for possession of and dealing in drugs

Offence	Type of trial	Class under Misuse of Drugs Act		
		A	B	C
Possession	Summary	6 months + £2,000 fine	3 months + £500 fine	3 months + £200 fine
	Indictment	7 years + unlimited fine	5 years + unlimited fine	2 years + unlimited fine
'Trafficking'	Summary	6 months + £2,000 fine	6 months + £2,000 fine	3 months + £500 fine
	Indictment	Life + unlimited fine	14 years + unlimited fine	5 years + unlimited fine

Table 3   A selected directory of controlled drugs

Class	Schedule	Drugs
B	2	Amphetamine
B	3	Amylobarbitone (Amytal)
B	3	Barbiturates
C	4	Benzodiazepines
B	3	Butobarbitone (Soneryl)
B	1	Cannabis and cannabis resin
C	4	Chlordiazepoxide (Librium)
A	2 and 5	Cocaine
B	2 and 5	Codeine (Actified, Phensedyl)
B	2	Dexamphetamine (Dexedrine)
A	2	Dextromoramide (Palfium)
C	2 and 5	Dextropropoxyphene (Distalgesic)
C	4	Diazepam (Valium)
C	3	Diethylpropion (Tenuate)
B	2 and 5	Dihydrocodeine (DF 118)
A	2	Dipipanone (Diconal)
A	2	Fentanyl
C	4	Flurazepam (Dalmane)
B	2	Glutethimide
A	2	Heroin
A	2	Levomethorphan
A	2	Levomoramide
C	4	Lorazepam (Ativan)
A	1	LSD, lysergamide
C	3	Meprobamate (Equanil)
A	2	Methadone (Physeptone)
B	2	Methaqualone
B	2	Methylamphetamine
B	2	Methylphenidate (Ritalin)
A	2 and 5	Morphine
C	4	Nitrazepam (Mogadon)
A	2 and 5	Opium, medicinal

Table 3   A selected directory of controlled drugs *continued*

Class	Schedule	Drugs
A	1	Opium, raw
C	4	Oxazepam (Serenid)
B	3	Pentazocine (Fortral)
B	3	Pentobarbitone (Nembutal)
A	2	Pethidine (Pamergan)
B	2	Phenmetrazine
C	3	Phentermine
A	1	Psilocin and related compounds, found in liberty cap mushrooms
B	3	Quinalbarbitone (Seconal)
C	4	Temazepam (Euhypnos)
C	4	Triazolam (Halcion)

Drugs are listed in alphabetical order of their non-proprietary name. Common trade (or proprietary) names of those marketed for medical use in the UK are given in brackets.

Assessing the Relative Dangers of Drugs

As we shall see, the law classifies drugs according to their supposed dangers and allocates penalties for possession and trafficking. It is questionable whether this classification is entirely rational but that is how the law is. Another approach to the problem is to consider first the personal hazards of drug use and then the social hazards. Two such classifications have been suggested in the USA. The first classifies them according to individual hazards, as follows:

1 Very high individual hazard rating: alcohol, barbiturates and non-barbiturate sedatives; central stimulants.
2 High individual hazard rating: minor tranquillizers, phencyclidine and hashish.

3 Intermediate individual hazard rating: heroin, cocaine, methadone, tobacco, cigarettes, codeine and opium.
4 Low individual hazard rating: marijuana and caffeine.
5 Very low individual hazard rating: cigars, coffee and tea.

The second classification has ranked psychoactive drugs in order of their potential hazards to society. The ranking, though controversial, certainly is of interest:

1 Alcohol.
2 Sedatives and hypnotics.
3 Central stimulants.
4 Heroin.
5 Volatile solvents.
6 Cigarettes.
7 LSD.
8 Marijuana.

It is interesting to note that alcohol is thereby regarded as the most hazardous drug to society at large – and it is perfectly legal!

The hazards to society as defined in this classification include causing social apathy, driving accidents, aggressive behaviour, violence and suicide.

Thus we see that neither of these classifications is entirely satisfactory and that there are inconsistencies. This perhaps reflects our lack of understanding of many of the problems relating to drug abuse.

Drugs and Delinquency

Society shows little tolerance for drug-taking – weary acceptance might sum up the contemporary attitude. People tend to make value judgements about drug takers since they are regarded unfavourably by society even if this unfavourable view is sugared by the word 'sick'. Too often they are regarded as being responsible for criminal acts supposedly triggered off by drug use. There is still a popular belief that drugs cause people to behave violently, to commit sexual excesses and to allow their moral standards to deteriorate. These beliefs can be reinforced by the media and by incautious pronouncements by badly informed public figures.

The relationship of delinquent behaviour to drug use is complex so before reviewing particular issues involved, a few aspects of delinquent behaviour are summarized.

A crime is regarded as taking place 'when a society with recognized ways of behaving or when a part of society which has power and authority to do so categorizes certain varieties of extreme or damaging behaviour as being liable to punishment'. The incidence and prevalence of crime in any country are provided by official agencies which record criminal statistics. In Britain offences are divided into two groups, indictable and non-indictable. Non-indictable offences are common and include drunkenness, taking and driving away motor vehicles, dangerous driving and certain sexual offences. In the United Kingdom approximately 60 per cent of the total number of offences dealt with by the courts are motoring offences, yet public attention is constantly directed to the increase in delinquent and violent behaviour among young people.

In Britain delinquent behaviour must be seen against the general social background of the country. Britain is mainly a single-culture nation with a more or less stratified society. There is little organized crime and the historical and economic climate has been one of gradual social development influenced by moderate radicalism. The welfare state produced a new range of opportunities for self-betterment and on the whole a modestly acceptable degree of equality of educational opportunity. Unhappily, in recent years this situation has changed considerably for the worse with the increase in unemployment and the erosion of the concept of the welfare state. There has been a steady increase in juvenile offences since the Second World War. There was a sharp rise from immediately after the war up to 1951, little change between 1951 and 1957, and thereafter a renewed increase.

The main age group involved in the increase tended to be that between sixteen and twenty-one but the peak age of conviction remains at around fourteen or fifteen. By the age of twenty-five the number convicted is half that of youngsters aged fourteen.

The main problems of delinquency concern young boys. The factors contributing to such delinquent behaviour are numerous and the evidence for their relevance is at times conflicting. One must be cautious about accepting figures provided by official agencies. Recorded increases in offences may be affected by a number of factors. There may be changes in the reporting patterns used by the police, or the public may be more ready to report certain offences, particularly violent ones. Victims of assault tend nowadays to report the offence more readily than formerly.

There is a clear sex difference in delinquent behaviour. The ratio of male to female offenders is of the order of six to one, and decreases with age. In England the main offences involving women are shoplifting, prostitution and assaults against other women and children. Also, crimes committed by women may occur in the context of a special relationship and never be reported, e.g. the prostitute's client who has his money stolen would normally be reluctant to report the offence. The main offences committed by juveniles in the United Kingdom are minor larcenies, taking and driving away, damage to property and absconding. Juvenile offences are most common in larger cities and a broad picture of the typical juvenile offender has been drawn. Much stress is laid on the frequency with which such youngsters come from 'broken homes'. In this context divorce or separation is of greater significance than the death of one parent.

There is no correlation between delinquency and intelligence but youngsters studied tend to show low educational attainment. This is probably because they are likely to come from a domestic background where family expectations are low and little interest is taken in their future prospects. The one quite clear factor is that juvenile delinquency is disproportionately high in slum areas and there is a real correlation between delinquency and both poverty in a material sense and poverty of expectation in a more subtle sense. Clearly in the present British socio-economic situation one can expect a continued rise in delinquent behaviour.

Another important point is that delinquent youngsters tend to come from large, unsupervised families. Being a member of a large family means that a youngster can easily drift into delinquency

44

without any adequate supervision. Even if the parents are earning a reasonably good wage, supporting a large family is bound to strain their economy. This was the case in times of full employment; with the continued high unemployment rate the situation has naturally worsened. In recent years violent crime has shown a disturbing rate of increase; particularly violent crime against women.

There is no single cause for criminal behaviour. Numerous studies have looked at the social backgrounds, personal characteristics, psychological attitudes and so on of youngsters involved in criminal acts, and certain general observations have emerged. But it must be conceded that with the exception of the age and sex factors mentioned earlier, no single factor could be used to predict criminal behaviour. No single type of disability has a monopoly in relation to delinquency; it seems that delinquent people undergo a series of adverse pressures of one sort or another which edge them into criminality.

Returning to drug use and criminality, the drug taker has in the past been credited with a wide range of anti-social behaviour caused by the influence of drugs – the so-called 'dope fiend'. This myth has been reinforced and popularized by fiction but has little substance in reality. An excellent example of this comes from the report of the Indian Hemp Drugs Commission of 1893, which examined a large number of witnesses concerning the physical, moral and mental effects of taking hashish. In a general conclusion the Commission reported that although many witnesses claimed to have seen violent crimes committed under the influence of hashish, when questioned none of them was able to remember any precise details.

Clearly a person who has aggressive tendencies is more likely to behave aggressively when under the influence of certain substances, particularly alcohol. There is a high correlation between alcohol and violent crimes just as there is between alcohol and road traffic accidents. Overall, 50 per cent of the world's road traffic accidents involve alcohol. People intoxicated by alcohol suffer impaired judgement and lowered self-control – and if they are basically touchy and irritable it is hardly surprising if they erupt into violence.

Opiates have the reverse effect. They tend to dull people's behaviour and decrease violent tendencies, sexual appetite and

45

thirst. Even as long ago as the 1920s an American psychiatrist suggested that aggressive psychopathic people would perhaps improve in temperament under the influence of opiates, and in parenthesis it may be said that for at least two hundred years opium was used by medical men as a tranquillizer, until its potential dangers were fully appreciated.

The USA has the largest problems of delinquency linked with drug use, and this is probably a consequence of repressive legislation rather than of drug use. The Harrison Act of 1914, which effectively abolished the lawful possession of heroin, had the indirect effect of putting all drug users automatically outside the law, and it intensified the reluctance of doctors and social agencies to have anything to do with them. The only way in which the drug user could obtain a drug such as heroin was illicitly, and over the years a most intricate system of marketing and distribution has developed with all the sophistication and complexity of a large industrial organization. An individual with a drug habit costing a hundred dollars a day will need that hundred dollars – and the simplest way to acquire it is by theft. Theft by drug users probably accounts for something like 70 per cent of the larcenies committed in New York City, and it is likely that every day several million dollars' worth of property is stolen to provide money to buy drugs. Violent acts do occur – not under the influence of a drug but under the indirect influence of the need to procure it. An established addict will go to any lengths to obtain drugs, particularly if he or she happens also to have an anti-social personality disorder. It is no understatement to say that repressive anti-drug legislation in the USA has contributed to a major social disaster by intensifying the problems of criminality. Even if heroin were to be made available to addicts there it would probably make little or no impression. So immense is the extent of the problem it would probably be too little and too late.

Research workers in Merseyside in England quite clearly demonstrated a close relationship between extensive heroin use amongst young unemployed adults and unusually high rates of theft. The heroin users become involved in a criminal lifestyle in which drug use and crime are closely related. It has been shown too in the Wirral, a part of Merseyside, that there is an identifiable section of youngsters whose social and economic situation edges them to the margins of society, to become the so-called under-class. Custodial prison sentences have been ineffective in rehabilitating such youngsters and there is an obvious need for longer-term solutions based in the community. In the Wirral it has been clearly demonstrated that there has been an exceptional rise in domestic burglaries – 260 per cent since 1980 compared with a national increase of about 90 per cent. And this rise is a result of the criminality of several hundred of the area's daily heroin users. Again, in Merseyside it has been shown that drug users treated in the Liverpool Drug Dependency Clinic were responsible for crimes amounting to about £7 million a year to support their drug habits before being taken on at the Clinic.

AIDS

The Acquired Immunodeficiency Syndrome was first discovered in 1981 in homosexual males. It was next found amongst intravenous drug users and Haitians; thereafter among people who had received transfusions of blood or blood products, children born to infected mothers, and heterosexual partners of AIDS sufferers. In 1983 it was found among Africans.

In 1983 the virus that caused the disorder, the Human Immunodeficiency Virus (HIV), was discovered and the specific routes by which the disorder is transmitted were gradually mapped out. Intravenous drug users are highly at risk in Europe and the USA. For example, in the USA 25 per cent of all cases have occurred in people who are self-injectors.

Sexual transmission of HIV is the prime route, however, and it is transmitted by both homosexual and heterosexual activity. In the USA and Britain homosexual males remain the biggest risk group. At present about 75 per cent of US adult males with AIDS are homosexual or bisexual men, about 8 per cent of these being self-injectors. So for the drug user, there is an extremely high risk of HIV infection by the use of shared needles. This has been demonstrated particularly in Scotland.

47

The transmission of AIDS appears to be associated with
repeated exposure. In other words, the highly promiscuous homosexual or heterosexual and the frequent self-injector.

AIDS – United Kingdom

AIDS is a most unusual disorder not just because of its immensely
high mortality rate (probably 100 per cent) but also because it has
produced a considerable reaction, at times amounting to panic, in
society in general. From the beginning much of the media coverage
of AIDS has been grossly inaccurate. In the *Reader's Digest* there
was a feature entitled 'Aids – The Plague of Fear'. The fear of this
dreadful disease has engendered the motion that it is highly con-
tagious, despite all evidence to the contrary.

By 1986 approximately 90 per cent of patients with AIDS in the
United Kingdom had been involved in either homosexual or
bisexual activity. In England and Wales, out of 2,081 HIV antibody-
positive people, only 54 were self-injectors. In Scotland, however,
503 out of 795 were self-injectors, and of these 482 came from
Edinburgh.

The epidemic of HIV infection appears to have started in Edinburgh among self-injectors who were heterosexuals. What is of
interest is that the Edinburgh epidemic was peculiar to that particular city in Scotland. For instance, the level of HIV-positive
reactions in self-injectors in Dundee was 39 per cent, in Glasgow
4.5 per cent and in England and Wales only 10 per cent. These
figures refer, it should be reiterated, to self-injectors. However,
there are regional differences elsewhere; for instance in the USA,
where 17 per cent of AIDS patients are self-injectors, the proportion of self-injecting AIDS sufferers in New York is 72 per cent as
opposed to 2 per cent in California. The high percentage of drug
users among HIV positives in Edinburgh is therefore unusual, but
not unique.

The proportion of self-injecting drug users among the HIV-
positive population ranges from 20 to 76 per cent in Europe
depending on the country concerned. Nevertheless there are les-
sons to be learned from this finding since, in Edinburgh, needles and
syringes became unavailable to addicts after 1981. The police are

said to have searched pharmacies and destroyed syringes and needles subsequently discovered. Thereafter retail pharmacies were unwilling to supply self-injectors with needles and syringes and so syringe-sharing became the rule. If an addict could obtain a needle and syringe he or she would share with up to forty people in a day in the so-called 'shooting galleries'. In these gatherings equipment was handed from one person to another. Self-reports from self-injectors reveal that 42 per cent of Edinburgh self-injectors shared needles and syringes every day and 63 per cent every week, as opposed to 14 per cent or 30 per cent of south London self-injectors. Further support for this high sharing rate was provided by the high rate of hepatitis B sero-positivity (between 60 and 80 per cent of self-injectors) plus the obvious expected increase in infective disorders such as endocarditis, pneumonia and skin infections.

Yet in the face of all this evidence of the folly of suppressing needle availability there is still a strong body of opinion against giving needles and syringes to addicts on the basis that it might encourage others who are not injecting to start doing so. AIDS is a major health threat which is much more dangerous than drug addiction. To date it is untreatable and seems likely to remain so for years.

International Control of Narcotic Drugs

The control of narcotic drugs is a detailed topic but there are a few points that need to be mentioned since they are frequently misunderstood.

The history of international co-operation in achieving effective control of narcotic drugs began in 1909 when an international conference took place in Shanghai. The main topic of discussion was the problem of the control of opium in China. In 1912 the Hague Convention agreed that the suppression of opium smoking should be enforced and that narcotics should be manufactured strictly for medical usage only. In 1920, 1924 and in 1925 when the Geneva Convention was signed the whole problem of international control was formalized and at the present time countries all over the world operate through the United Nations a mutually agreed system of control of these drugs.

In 1961 the United Kingdom was one of the signatories of the Single Convention on Narcotic Drugs, a further step in rationalizing the procedure. Cannabis is included in the Single Convention as it was in the 1925 Convention, a point that needs to be taken into consideration when the question of legalizing cannabis is under discussion.

Legal control of drug use throughout the world

There are a number of international agreements aimed at controlling drug use, such as the Hague Convention and the Single Convention. The question is, how effective have these controls been? The demand for illicit drugs such as heroin, marijuana and cocaine is so great, and hence also the profits to be made from trafficking, that not even the most stringent penalties seem to make any difference at all. Throughout the world thirteen countries carry the death penalty for certain types of drug offences, mainly involving heroin, and six countries carry the death penalty for the possession or sale of marijuana. The worldwide epidemic of drug addiction which has taken place in the last twenty-plus years is a reality not a myth. The enormous sums of money which change hands lead people to take great risks, undeterred by the penalties they may face.

The US government has talked about 'a war on drugs' and has adopted a military style operation against drug smugglers from South America, but with little real effect despite the accounts of huge seizures. It seems that as one huge seizure is made another consignment is already emplaned. It must be asked, therefore, whether maintaining this sort of attempt at control is really worth the effort. Would it not be better and more rational to acknowledge that people will intoxicate themselves come what may and to offer some sort of a compromise? For instance, we know that cigarette smoking is the major preventable cause of death in the Western world, yet no one would seriously consider totally banning cigarettes, although cigarette smoking is highly dangerous. This is not to suggest that heroin and other drugs should be made freely available but rather that they should be more available on a legal basis than they are at present. This argument is shunned by people who do not care to consider its possible force. Prohibition of alcohol in the USA was a major social disaster, creating huge empires of crime which have since flourished and, of course, moved on to the illicit sale, import and distribution of narcotics. The lesson seems clear. Prohibition effectively established organized crime with such an immense industrial and power base that, after the Second World War, one of its leaders was able to boast, 'we are bigger than US Steel'. It is questionable whether syndicated crime would have achieved such an immense diversity of activity and influence had it not been for the major thrust that was given to it by the prohibition of alcohol.

Any politician who wishes to make political capital can do so by declaring 'war on drugs'. The most extreme examples involve capital punishment. A sound example of the way in which capital punishment has failed regarding drug dependence comes from Iran. Both before and after the revolution the extent of heroin addiction in Iran was staggering. To try to deal with this the Ayatollah Khalkhali ordered that any heroin addicts apprehended would receive the death penalty, and indeed many did. It was estimated that there were three million heroin addicts in Iran, i.e one in twelve of the population – a truly astonishing figure. However, having enforced the death penalty, the Ayatollah himself abandoned it after a time – since the numbers involved were so great that even he must have realized that the policy was getting nowhere.

At the end of it all one is left with the inescapable conclusion that it is virtually impossible to deter people from intoxicating themselves with whatever they choose to take and, if this is the case, that it must be better for the substances to come from a lawful source rather than from illicit sources who gain profit, fight battles – literally – with each other and emerge usually unscathed. This is not to suggest free hand-outs of drugs to everyone; far from it. It is merely to suggest that since the hard-line approach is palpably unworkable – as would be a free market – there must be something of a middle of the road approach, for in the case of drugs it is all too clear that crime *does* pay.

4

Legal Drugs of Abuse:
Alcohol and Tobacco

Alcohol Dependence

Alcoholism is regarded as a disease; formerly it was regarded as a vice or some form of moral turpitude. It is convenient to regard it as a disease since it produces immense physical, psychological and social disabilities, though some prefer not to regard it as such on the grounds that the illness concept provides the problem drinker with an escape hatch from bearing responsibility for his or her acts. The arguments for and against are given in more detail on page 90 *et seq.*

Ethyl alcohol (ethanol) is made by a process of fermentation. The fermentation ceases when the yeast runs out. The alcohol level can then be increased by distillation. The alcohol level in beer is around 4 per cent, in table wines from 8 per cent to 14 per cent, and in spirits from 35 to 40 per cent. People use alcohol because it makes them feel relaxed and disinhibited, and produces mild euphoria. Unfortunately, it does not stop there: as the blood alcohol level rises so the person becomes more socially unacceptable in behaviour, ultimately becoming drowsy and, if sufficient quantities are consumed, possibly passing into coma and death.

The disinhibiting effects of alcohol may be socially acceptable in that a person who finds it difficult to socialize may find this easier after consuming a small quantity of alcohol. Unhappily, further consumption makes matters worse – with drunkenness, loutish behaviour and violence, even homicide.

What is alcoholism?

The World Health Organization defined alcoholism in 1952: alcoholics were those 'excessive drinkers whose dependence on alcohol has attained such a degree that it shows a noticeable mental disturbance or an interference with their bodily and mental health, their interpersonal relations and social functioning; or those who show the prodromal [early] signs of such development'.

Many feel, however, that this definition is perhaps not far reaching enough, and there is a tendency today to use the term alcoholism as a generic term, and talk about 'problem drinking'. This is probably a good idea since most alcohol-dependent people find it very difficult to accept the idea of being labelled as alcoholic but can cope with the label 'problem drinker'. One thing is certain and that is that alcohol dependence is related to the amount consumed each day. In 1971 it was stated in one study that anyone consuming more than eight pints of beer or fifteen measures of spirits a day was alcohol dependent. This gross underestimate has now been revised. Dosage is measured in units – a unit being a half pint of beer, a glass of wine or a single measure of spirits. The weekly limits are twenty-one units for men and fourteen for women. Anyone who exceeds that dose is a problem drinker and at risk of the complications of alcohol abuse. Using the 'unit' dose is simple and may be psychologically less painful for drinkers to handle.

Perhaps the most useful way of looking at the question of 'alcoholism' is to adopt the description of alcohol dependence given by Professor Griffith Edwards and Dr M. M. Grosse in 1976.[1] Their approach was to abandon the notion of a rigid definition of alcohol dependence and to look at the ways in which it could be identified, for which they used a number of quite simple markers. These make very good sense:

1 The dependent drinker develops a narrow repertoire of alcohol consumption; a non-dependent drinker drinks for a variety of reasons, and so the amount consumed varies from day to day. But

1. G. Edwards and M. M. Grosse (1976) 'Alcohol dependence: provisional description of a clinical syndrome', *British Medical Journal*, Vol. 1, pp. 1058–61.

the dependent drinker uses alcohol to avoid withdrawal symptoms and the consumption of alcohol becomes more or less fixed upon this basis.

2 Drinking occupies the person's activities to the exclusion of pretty much everything else. For instance, the dependent alcohol user will steal, beg money and borrow in order to obtain drink.

3 The person develops withdrawal symptoms, including trembling, fear, severe insomnia, nightmares and hallucinations.

4 Tolerance occurs so that the dependent person consumes alcohol to an extent which would probably render an ordinary person completely incapable.

5 Using alcohol to relieve withdrawal symptoms: this is seen in the person who has to have a drink upon waking in the morning because he or she knows that this will relieve the feelings of illness he or she is enduring.

6 Dependent alcohol users realize that they cannot control alcohol consumption.

7 Finally, there is the relapse after abstinence. More often than not a dependent alcohol user finds it quite easy to quit drinking, but a return to minimal alcohol consumption soon leads to dependent use.

Psychological dependence on alcohol is probably much more common than people realize. Many normal social drinkers will feel a relatively strong need to take one or two drinks in the evening but not exceed that dose. If this remains the case, such psychological dependence is not really very important. The problem arises, however, if consumption of alcohol begins steadily to increase, leading to the appearance of symptoms indicating loss of control of drinking. These symptoms include lying to oneself and others about the amount drunk, being preoccupied with alcohol and with keeping more than adequate supplies handy, and taking extra drinks before going to parties, say, or undergoing some type of psychological ordeal. Hangovers which lead to loss of work are a bad sign, and also the tendency to take drink earlier and earlier in the day even to the extent a person will drink in the middle of the night or even upon waking. Once drinking is out of control dependence becomes worse and the person experiences blackouts, memory gaps, early morning shakes – indicating physical withdrawal symptoms, and alcohol will often be taken to relieve the shakes. They will experience feelings of nausea and faintness with weakness upon standing, general tremulousness and a tendency to suffer from sustained depressive spells for no particular reason, combined with tearfulness. At this stage feelings of remorse and guilt about drinking may be prominent and the person may make genuine efforts to quit but usually to little avail.

As might be expected, psychological, social and occupational complications of alcohol use now appear. The individual's marital relationship will deteriorate as a wife is constantly sickened and exhausted by the loutish behaviour of her husband when drunk, and also because of his lack of affection and sexual drive caused by excessive alcohol. In addition, work performance falls off, more and more time is lost from work, quarrels develop with employers and colleagues and the individual may soon be out of a job. Other social complications which may have disastrous consequences include drunken driving, possibly leading to the killing of innocent people, getting into fights and generally indulging in violent, even homicidal, behaviour. Alcohol is clearly implicated in homicide in the United Kingdom and the USA in a substantial percentage of cases. Suicide attempts are common in alcoholism, and alcohol may be implicated in 30 to 40 per cent of suicide attempts in Britain. It all presents a sorry picture and when one takes into account that there are around half a million alcoholic patients in Britain the extent of the problem will be appreciated. For instance, as long ago as 1977 the financial loss in industrial output through alcoholism was estimated at £500 million and the cost to health and social services around £52 million. Clearly this is a major public health problem and it must be emphasized that alcohol abuse is the most important and serious variety of drug abuse affecting our society. It far outstrips heroin.

The physical complications of alcoholism are extensive. The problem drinker is more likely to become diabetic and to suffer from disorders such as pancreatitis, and the alcohol abuser is much more at risk from chronic obstructive lung disease because of associated heavy smoking. High blood pressure and an increased incidence of coronary heart disease are also associated with severe alcohol abuse.

Liver damage begins in a mild way and is reversible if a person quits drinking, but prolonged alcohol abuse causes permanent liver damage and cirrhosis occurs leading to liver failure and death. The alcoholic is also more at risk of the development of duodenal ulcers, inflammation of the stomach (gastritis) and is affected with retching and vomiting in the morning when the alcohol withdrawal symptoms develop. Profuse sweating and severe sleep disturbance are other important features.

In establishing the diagnosis of heavy drinking a useful tactic is to ask the person to describe a typical day in his or her life. This usually elicits a more accurate history of how much alcohol is consumed than asking the bald question, 'How much do you drink?'

The causes of alcoholism

Alcohol abuse is more common in men than in women, the approximate ratio being four to one, but it is becoming more common in women. This is of particular importance since the recognition of the fetal alcohol syndrome, which occurs in pregnant women. Even small quantities of alcohol consumed in pregnancy can lead to severe mental retardation and other abnormalities in offspring.

National drinking habits change with time; the heavy spirits drinking in eighteenth- and nineteenth-century England produced few moderate drinkers: people either drank heavily or not at all, and this excessive consumption of alcohol in vast quantities led to the formation of the Temperance Movement.

Certain cultures are more at risk than others: in the United Kingdom the Irish and the Scots lead the field. Psychiatric admissions for alcoholism are four times greater in Scotland than in England. In the USA the Irish and the northern Europeans are heavily represented in the alcoholic population but the Scots are mysteriously absent. Again, in the USA the Black American is highly represented – but is this an ethnic or an economic association? Jews and Muslims are practically invulnerable to alcoholism. This is because Jews are educated to use alcohol in a sensible and formal fashion, and in the case of Islam there is a total ban on its consumption.

Transcultural studies reveal national differences in drinking habits. Beverage choice varies: in the USA and the United Kingdom people prefer to drink beer and spirits, while in Italy, Spain and France wine is the main drink.

Occupation is an important factor. People in the liquor industry are highly at risk, as are those in jobs where alcohol may be used as a business lubricant. This is also true for people whose jobs are full of tension and competition, easily soothed by a quick drink – which soon becomes more than one. Doctors are a high-risk group.

Psychiatric disorders associated with alcoholism

A number of clearly defined psychiatric illnesses are associated with alcoholism. The most commonly known is delirium tremens in which the person develops a state of clouded consciousness and may become very agitated and terrified, experiencing hallucinations. This may occur after a prolonged drinking bout or after a period of enforced abstention. There are other less common disorders, all of which involve brain damage and severe memory impairment; a good example is the so-called Korsakov psychosis, in which the person loses awareness of time and place for recent events and confabulates answers to questions. Alcoholics can develop acute paranoid disorders, usually in a setting of sexual jealousy; this may well be related to the loss of sexual potency in the alcoholic.

Finally alcohol abuse can cause permanent organic brain damage, which is irreversible and characterized by progressive intellectual impairment, failure of recent memory and general deterioration. If the person abstains from alcohol the disorder will not progress but the patient will be left with a degree of permanent brain damage. It is now considered that permanent brain damage from alcohol is far more common than had previously been realized, and that the safe dosage level of alcohol is really much lower than had previously been thought.

Recognition of the problem drinker

It is easy enough to recognize the extent of the problem where the person comes to see the physician. However, problem drinkers can often be overlooked by doctors because they present with physical illnesses related to their alcoholic problem yet do not mention their alcohol consumption. Take, for instance, the patient who presents

57

with recurrent attacks of abdominal pain caused by gastritis. Such a patient may not mention alcohol at all. It is therefore important for the doctor and others involved always to consider this as an underlying cause. The specific medical complications of alcohol, as previously described, are thus important landmarks for doctors and those working in the field to look out for. Simple social markers such as drink/driving offences, absenteeism from work on Mondays, and increasingly frequent absenteeism for unspecified minor illnesses are all important points to take into consideration.

Usually a person attending a clinic for the management of alcohol problems will be assessed not only by a psychiatrist but also by social workers and psychologists. The whole problem will usually be assessed with the patient's family to determine the impact of the problem on family members. Thereafter the usual goal is to seek abstention. The majority of people find it hard to accept the idea of total abstention for ever when presented to them immediately. Some authorities feel that it is worthwhile striving for a period of abstention of three months, at the end of which time the person will have learned just how big a place alcohol has been taking in his or her life, and will become more able to look honestly at the ramifications of excessive drinking. At the present time there is controversy surrounding the problem of whether people can return to controlled drinking. Undoubtedly some can but it would be a brave person who would say that everyone can, and so for the moment this is something that is under review.

The management of the alcoholic's problems immediately after he or she has committed himself or herself to entering a programme will start with a decision whether the person should enter hospital to undergo withdrawal or whether this can be done on a day-attendance basis. The latter procedure is finding increasing favour. During the withdrawal process the person will receive medication, usually in the form of chlordiazepoxide (Librium), on a four-hourly basis for period of a few days in order to avoid withdrawal distress including fits and delirium in severe cases. While this is going on the person will receive counselling and support from all concerned.

Group counselling and group psychotherapy are the favourite methods in use. Their object is to encourage the alcohol abuser to look at his or her problems honestly and share distress, anguish etc. with the group, and as it were learn to look at those problems through the eyes of other people who have been through remarkably similar experiences. This is really the fundamental approach – perhaps modified according to particular taste – which is used by most treatment programmes. Any form of long-term medication using mind-altering drugs is really inappropriate since it is likely to replace one form of dependence with another. Other pharmacological methods such as the use of disulfiram (Antabuse) can be used though many people would regard them as a last resort. Disulfiram causes intense physical distress and collapse if the individual takes any alcohol. At one time it was felt to be the 'wonder drug' in the treatment of alcohol problems but it has not really lived up to that promise.

Alcoholics should be offered membership of Alcoholics Anonymous (AA). This organization, founded in America by two ex-alcoholics, has given help to a vast number of alcoholics: probably more than from 'official' treatment sources. It is founded on self-help and acknowledgement of disability. The AA member can count on help at any time from other members and the AA meetings combine *esprit de corps* with commitment in the shape of a shared problem. Members commit themselves to twelve steps to recovery and acknowledge the help of a 'higher power'. Ultimately, however, whatever treatment method is used, the responsibility and choice and determination of the individual concerned will carry the day.

The question of return to controlled social drinking has been mentioned before. This is a contentious topic and first came up some years ago in Finland and in Britain where separately it was reported that a percentage of long-term alcoholic patients had been able to return to rational controlled social drinking. Although this view has never been accepted by Alcoholics Anonymous, which regards total permanent abstention as the only possible goal, it does seem that a proportion of people can achieve this. It is done by preceding entry into the programme by a period of abstention of, say, six months or longer. The therapist decides upon a programme of controlled drinking activity. For instance, someone might be told that he or she should remain abstinent from alcohol throughout the week but could have one drink at lunchtime on Saturday and one in the evening, and possibly another on the Sunday. In the author's personal experience it is encouraging to have met people who have been able to handle this sort of programme, but it must be emphasized that it is regarded with extreme disfavour by many highly reputable authorities in the field. Time will show.

Alcohol absorption

Alcohol is unique among drugs of abuse in that it does not have to be digested but is absorbed straight into the bloodstream from the stomach and small gut. About four-fifths of the alcohol is absorbed in the small intestine. Absorption is influenced in a number of ways, the first being tolerance. Those who have been drinking for many years need more alcohol to experience any effect than normal drinkers. The amount of food present in the stomach is important since food delays alcohol absorption. The speed at which drinks are consumed is again important; gulping drinks elevates the blood alcohol level very quickly. The more alcohol drunk, the quicker does the blood alcohol level rise.

Alcohol is broken down in the liver and excreted in the urine and in the lungs.

General points about alcohol use

The majority of people who drink alcohol do not become alcohol dependent, nevertheless caution is needed to try to prevent the development of this type of disorder. People need to be educated in how alcohol should be consumed and this education ought perhaps to begin very early in life since alcohol use is so prevalent.

There are a number of simple rules. People should be encouraged to drink alcohol slowly, to avoid drinking on an empty stomach, to try to set limits and always dilute spirits with either water or mineral water (this will no doubt be greeted with derision by Scottish readers). Other good rules are to avoid using alcohol as a form of stress-relieving substance, and to determine one's limits of alcohol usage.

People should also be educated on how to use alcohol when entertaining guests. Drinks should not be forced upon them – a plentiful supply of soft drinks should be available and people should be encouraged to eat. Other varieties of entertainment at a party should be available so that people can be diverted from drinking too much.

The prevention of alcohol-related disability can be started in a simple way. However, other measures at a wider level are needed. In the first place there should be a complete ban on the advertising of alcoholic beverages. Next comes the question of taxation. At a simplistic level it is easy to say that raising the tax on alcohol will help but this could be construed as a middle-class way of getting round the problem since the middle classes can afford the cost of increased revenue. The working classes and the unemployed probably could not, and it is questionable whether the middle classes should take it upon themselves to impose their own standards of 'morality' on those less fortunate. However, the idea of an increased tax has merit.

Tobacco

Tobacco is the most commonly consumed drug in Britain. Forty per cent of the population over the age of sixteen smoke: 45 per cent of men and about 34 per cent of women over sixteen smoke although there is evidence that women are smoking more than formerly.

The only legal constraints on smoking are that it is against the law to sell cigarettes or tobacco products to people under sixteen and that cigarettes may not be advertised on television. Otherwise there are no restrictions on the use of these addictive and highly dangerous substances.

Smoking might be described as 'the innocent addiction' in that people take it up at quite an early age, e.g. around thirteen and are genuinely unaware of its addictive potential. It is a classic example of learned behaviour in psychological terms, in that each time people smoke they experience a reward, i.e. a pleasurable effect which conditions them to carry on and consume increasing quantities of tobacco. The main effects that people find pleasurable are the lowering of tension, a slight mood elevation and some stimulation of mental energy.

In trying to determine an individual person's pattern of smoking behaviour one looks at a number of factors. First, does the person crave cigarettes? – craving is always difficult to overcome. Second, how much of their smoking behaviour is pure habit linked to certain routine daily activities? Some smokers report stimulation, others report relief of tension and a general feeling of relaxation; but the pattern is not necessarily the same with everyone. Others will stress the importance of cigarette handling and all the paraphernalia that go with cigarettes, such as lighters etc. The substances that cause the 'pleasurable' effects in smoking are predominantly nicotine and carbon monoxide. These substances, together with other constituents of tobacco smoke such as tar, make smoking one of the most potent public health hazards of the age. For instance, smokers in general have a higher standardized mortality rate than non-smokers at any age. Their life expectancy is less than that of non-smokers, and they are at higher risk from cancers in the mouth, pharynx and throat and oesophagus. They are more liable to suffer from arterial disease such as arteriosclerosis and disorders affecting main blood vessels in the arms and legs (Buerger's disease). In general the smoker's health is poorer in a non-specific way. Investigations have revealed that smokers are more susceptible to minor ailments such as flu and show a higher rate of absenteeism from work than non-smokers. Fertility can be impaired by smoking, and perhaps more striking is the finding that smoking mothers produce babies of lower birth weight and are more likely to produce premature babies. The most striking health hazard of smoking is lung cancer, which accounts for 40,000 deaths a year in Britain. It is beyond question that smoking cigarettes and tobacco products in any form is the prime cause of lung cancer despite the protests of mischievous people who try to play this down. In addition the smoker is much more at risk from coronary heart disease (CHD), which is the most common cause of death in Britain, and obstructive lung disease such as emphysema and chronic bronchitis. There is no doubt about the real health hazards associated with smoking.

Public attitudes to smoking have changed considerably in recent years, given a lead by professional people, particularly doctors, who abruptly changed their smoking habits. Giving up smoking has become more popular though non-smoking is much more common in the higher socio-economic groups. If one were at a party attended by doctors and their families exclusively, with say a hundred people present, one would be unlikely to find more than one person smoking.

Protest groups of non-smokers have become more vociferous. Movements such as ASH (Action on Smoking and Health) in Britain and others in the USA have lobbied for the reduction of smoking in public places. This is reflected in the ways in which no-smoking areas are provided in restaurants and airlines restrict the number of smoking places on aircraft. It seems likely that the airlines would be happy to ban smoking completely in flight if they were all prepared to agree to it, because of the fire hazards.

Giving up smoking

For a number of reasons giving up smoking isn't easy. Since the habit is relatively highly prevalent in the population pressure on the individual to give up smoking is not so great, and the smoker is discouraged from giving up by other smokers and the omnipresence of cigarettes. However, the heavy smoker, i.e. smoking more than twenty cigarettes a day, can be given advice regarding risk reduction. For instance, those who must smoke are advised to smoke a filtered low-tar cigarette and smoke only one-third of its length, since the tar concentration increases the more the cigarette is smoked. They should be advised to inhale less, to take fewer puffs and in general to smoke fewer cigarettes every day. A cynical physician once remarked that one of the surest ways to persuade someone to give up smoking was for the person to need admission to a coronary care unit with acute chest pain. Smokers should decide whether they want to try gradual reduction or stop completely. The majority of people find it difficult to stop completely. Gradual reduction can be achieved by advising the person to smoke only at prescribed times, e.g. after a meal and on specific social occasions. Smoking should be discouraged later at night since nicotine contributes to insomnia.

There is no simple way which a person can stop smoking but a number of aims can be used. The National Cancer Institute in the USA has produced a useful guide, including straightforward advice that when a person is considering giving up smoking, he or she should first take a positive decision to stop and avoid the fears associated with quitting.

This book isn't intended as a guide to giving up smoking but the following advice is generally given, and this may be of interest.

1 Develop reasons for stopping.
2 Avoid buying large quantities of cigarettes.
3 Avoid carrying packets of cigarettes.
4 Work out the cost of smoking.
5 Decide well in advance on a day to give up.
6 In the run up to the day, improve your physical condition through exercise.
7 On the day throw away all cigarettes and associated paraphernalia and go to the dentist to have your teeth cleaned.
8 Celebrate giving up and reward yourself, say every day, for not smoking.
9 Spend as much time as possible in places where smoking is forbidden.
10 Drink lots of fruit juice and water. Avoid alcohol and coffee.
11 Stay outdoors as much as possible and mix with non-smokers.

Finally, a word about weight gain, which worries most people who give up smoking. They should always be advised that the dangers of weight gain are much less than the dangers of smoking.

Last of all we should reject completely the statement: 'Well, we've all got to die of something.' Of course we have but the argument carries no force in the face of the appalling health hazards of smoking.

5

Prescribed and Illicit Drugs

Many of the drugs described in this chapter, i.e. narcotics, hypno-sedatives and tranquillizers, have valid medical uses. However, their abuse potential is high, and dependence on hypnosedatives and tranquillizers usually starts in the course of treatment – a sort of innocent dependence. The abuse potential of tranquillizers has been recognized only in comparatively recent times and no doubt many thousands of people became dependent on them without realizing it. They certainly were not taking the pills to get high but found themselves increasing the dosage when the desired effect did not occur. Narcotics, as has been mentioned, have a vital part to play in the treatment of painful disorders. Therapeutic dependence can occur in people who may have been given too powerful a narcotic to relieve pain. It should be emphasized, however, that therapeutic dependence is relatively uncommon. It is mostly found in people with long-standing chronic painful disorders, who obtain pain relief but also find that they experience a high, and need to take more of the drug. Therapeutic addicts do not constitute an important social problem. Their management is usually a matter of sensible manipulation of the medication by the prescribing physician.

Narcotics

Narcotic drugs are powerful pain relievers or analgesics and are used in the treatment of severe pain, such as that following major surgery and also in painful terminal illness. In addition to their pain-relieving effect they produce euphoria. This is a state where the person's mood is not elated but is one of happiness and contentment. At the same time the person tends to feel drowsy.

The model narcotic drug was originally opium – a naturally occurring substance. Opium is obtained from the plant *Papaver somniferum*, the opium poppy.

The important narcotics include naturally occurring substances, e.g. opium, derivatives of such substances, and synthetic drugs.

In general the narcotic drugs are used in the relief of severe pain. Nowadays sophisticated methods of delivery have been developed, particularly in terminal cancer where a person can receive small intermittent doses, pumped into a vein. This relieves pain without impairing the person's consciousness, permitting a dignified exit from a painful existence and allowing the sufferer to enjoy the company of family and friends without being drugged into unconsciousness.

Opium is obtained from the opium poppy by two means: first, by opening the pod, draining out the fluid and drying it and, second, by extracting it directly from the opium plant. The most important purified derivative of opium is morphine, developed by the German pharmacologist Sertürner in the nineteenth century. It is the most frequently used pain-relieving drug of the opioid type. Codeine, also derived directly from opium, is used mainly in suppression of coughs but has some pain-relieving qualities.

The most important derivative of opium is diamorphine (heroin). This was synthesized in 1898 and its original purpose was to be used in the treatment of morphine addiction! Its addictive powers were not realized at first – a story which is repeated throughout the history of dependency-producing drugs.

Diamorphine has a short biological half-life (see page 86) so that the person who becomes dependent on it tends to need more and more doses to achieve the desired effect. This is initially one of euphoria but ultimately, when a person becomes severely dependent, the main use is to avoid withdrawal symptoms.

Synthetic opiate drugs include meperidine (pethidine), an analgesic which is used most frequently in the practice of midwifery to relieve labour pains. Methadone is another synthetic analgesic drug developed in Germany in the Second World War. It has the great advantage of a prolonged biological half-life and, as will be seen, has found a place in the treatment of diamorphine addiction.

Another commonly used synthetic is propoxyphene. This is quite widely used in Britain and does produce cases of dependency. Other synthetic opiate drugs include diconal, dipipanone and dextromoramide. All of the last four drugs are prepared in tablet form but are also misused by drugs users who crush them, dissolve them in water and inject them. So far as the self-injector is concerned, the main hazards are from injection due to unsterile self-injection or shared needles. These hazards outweigh the actual drug effect. A minority die from accidental overdose but the health hazards of self-injection are enormous in comparison.

Actions of opiates and opioid drugs

As previously stated the main actions are analgesic (pain relieving), sedative (depressing higher levels of central nervous system activity), and also the projection of euphoria, a state of mood change in which the person is neither elated nor depressed. Physical actions of the opioid drugs include inhibition of bowel movements, pupil constriction and nausea, often leading to vomiting. This latter effect is something that is lost quite speedily once tolerance is developed.

Psychiatric factors in opioid dependence

Numerous studies have indicated that a substantial proportion of heroin addicts are people either with personality disorders or in whom a former psychiatric disorder can diagnosed. The type of personality disorders encountered include anti-social (psychopathic) personality, immature personality, and people who have 'unclassified' personality disorders. In addition it was found that a small but significant proportion of heroin addicts are anxiety prone, or perhaps subject to bouts of depression which are poorly sustained but sufficient to warrant making a formal diagnosis. Other studies carried out on large groups of heroin users have involved the use of tests such as the General Health Questionnaire. This is a reliable and well-validated test which can determine the presence of psychiatric symptomatology in people and has been quite extensively used in population surveys in Britain, the USA and Canada. A typical such study indicated that approximately 50 per cent of a substantial series of heroin users scored sufficiently high on the test to be regarded as within the abnormal range. However, one must be cautious when interpreting and trying to determine the significance of such findings. Heroin usage is after all an uncommon disorder in the population and knowing of the dangers of drug usage one could predict that the people most likely become involved with drug usage would be high risk takers. This would certainly attract people with anti-social and immature personalities in whom the drug could give some degree of admittedly spurious comfort and support. Anxiety-prone and depressive people might also find solace in the drug, but clearly this does not account for all cases. In the early 1960s when the drug-dependence problem started becoming more extensive in Britain, it was clear that the majority of addicts seen at that time were on the whole quite disturbed. But this population seems to have been considerably diluted if one is to judge from present-day findings. Perhaps an analogy may be drawn here between drug dependence and smoking tobacco. When tobacco was first introduced in Britain it must have seemed to most people to be a quite extraordinary and unlikely thing for people to do. Inhaling the fumes and smoke from material smoked in a pipe is after all not a natural act. It may well be that the first smokers were a highly deviant group but as the habit spread right across the population normal people took it up! No one would for a moment suggest that all smokers have either personality problems or neurotic difficulties.

Hypnosedative Dependence

Introduction

Hypnosedative drugs induce sleep. They include the barbiturates and non-barbiturates. Properly speaking the tranquillizers should be included in this group because they have a similar type of action. However, although the hypnosedatives do include straightforward sleeping drugs such as the barbiturates and various tranquillizers, it is convenient to separate the two main groups.

The barbiturates

The term 'barbiturate' is a generic term applied to a group of drugs which are derived from barbituric acid. All these drugs depress higher brain activity, induce sleep and may relieve anxiety and tension. Depending on the biological half-life of the barbiturate concerned, so the duration of the action of the drug varies and for this reason barbiturates are categorized as being long acting, medium acting and short acting. Long-acting barbiturates include phenobarbitone (used mainly in the treatment of epilepsy); medium-acting barbiturates include amylobarbitone ('Amytal' and pentobarbitone ('Nembutal'); quinalbarbitone ('Seconal') is a short-acting barbiturate. The most rapidly acting barbiturates of all are those used in the induction of general anaesthesia, where an intravenous injection of thiopentone ('Pentothal') is given.

Since the barbiturates produce states of altered consciousness, drowsiness and sleep with relief of anxious feelings, it is hardly surprising that people become extremely dependent on them.

As it happens the widespread prescribing of barbiturates for sleep disorders is much less common in medical practice today, the dangers of these medications having been realized.

Clinical picture of barbiturate dependence

In barbiturate dependence psychological dependence is variable but physical dependence can be severe. However, the latter occurs only when dosage is maintained at levels well above the ordinary therapeutic levels.

Psychological dependence relates quite simply to the desirability of the drug effect – thus a tense person may easily become dependent on barbiturates since the drug relieves a distressing symptom and replaces it with a pleasant feeling. So the person repeats the dose throughout the day to produce the effect – just like alcohol.

People become very absorbed with drug taking, so that they are constantly reinforcing their doses. Chronic barbiturate takers present a picture which is very like that of chronic alcoholic intoxi-cation. They stagger about, their speech is slurred and often incom-prehensible. States of mental confusion and unusual mood disturbances with poor judgement are common.

Physical dependence on and chronic intoxication from barbiturates occurs in relatively small therapeutic doses, e.g. someone who takes a dosage of 400 mg a day for six weeks can show a typical picture of barbiturate intoxication, with psychological dependence, nausea, trembling and feelings of weakness and dizziness. In addition the person's blood pressure may fall when he or she stands (orthostatic hypotension). Ten per cent of such people taking this sort of dosage over a twelve-month period may develop withdrawal fits if the drug is abruptly stopped.

Barbiturate withdrawal symptoms

These start within twenty-four hours of discontinuing the medication and continue for a second or third day, though in the case of the longer-acting drugs severe symptoms do not appear until between the fourth and sixth day. Withdrawal symptoms include craving, trembling, feelings of anxiety, weakness, dizziness, withdrawal fits and states of delirium. The occurrence of fits in delirious states presents serious medical emergencies which, of all drug withdrawal states, are the most important since they can present a real hazard to life.

Patterns of barbiturate usage

In pre-tranquillizer days, the short-acting barbiturates were commonly used in the treatment of anxiety states and in such cases patients received small doses usually taken three times a day; for the majority of patients this probably led to little in the way of abuse since the practice was not to maintain the prescription of the drug for more than a few weeks. However, some patients remained on therapeutic doses for longer periods of time, and in many instances toleration of the drug occurred and they consumed larger and larger quantities, and developed chronic states of barbiturate intoxication. It should be realized that it was only in the 1950s that the syndrome of chronic barbiturate intoxication was described in the USA, and for years after that many doctors were totally unaware of its existence.

The author has in the past seen numerous patients who have become severely dependent and intoxicated in this way and who required in-patient detoxification. Such patients were predominantly middle-aged, neurotic individuals.

For many years opiate addicts used barbiturates for short-term relief when they were unable to obtain their drug of choice, and these were taken either by mouth or by crushing the tablets and injecting them; in itself a highly dangerous procedure. At the beginning of the drug dependence problem in the 1960s, in England – particularly in London – the majority of self-injecting heroin addicts used crushed barbiturate tablets by injection in times of withdrawal distress; the combination of these with self-injected central stimulant drugs such as methedrine produced very severe states of intoxication.

The medical uses of barbiturates at the present time are really limited to the use of phenobarbitone in the treatment of epilepsy, in which it has an honoured and established place. Doctors virtually discontinued prescribing barbiturates as sleeping pills once their dangers were properly understood. Insomnia is a troublesome symptom. It may be related to psychiatric disorders such as anxiety or depression, or to alcohol abuse, and most people as they grow older seem to require less sleep than formerly, though there is some disagreement about this.

The recommended management of insomnia today is to avoid the use of barbiturates, and also benzodiazepine tranquillizers since these can produce quite severe dependence later.

If it is possible to deal with an underlying psychiatric problem this will help the person's insomnia; otherwise simple advice is useful. A malted milk drink at bedtime is something people find palatable and useful, a gently playing radio or reading in bed can help the person to sleep. Another important cause of insomnia is cigarette smoking, and heavy smokers who cannot give up should be persuaded at least to cut down. Above all, too, the patient needs to be reminded that insomnia is not of itself a lethal disorder and that as long as one is lying down rather than pacing about, one will come to no harm.

Central Stimulant Drugs: the Amphetamines and Cocaine

The amphetamines

Introduction   The amphetamines first came into use in the 1930s when Myron Prinzmetal, a pharmacologist who later became a cardiologist, produced Benzedrine, the first of the amphetamine-type central stimulants. The amphetamines in general are related to ephedrine, a drug previously used in the treatment of asthma. At least fifty amphetamine or amphetamine-like medications are available, but their use in medical practice is severely restricted because of the dangers of abuse, dependence and psychosis.

The effects of amphetamines   The chief action of amphetamines is to stimulate the central nervous system so that the person becomes excited, restless and is unable to sleep. The person is talkative and feels cheery, has an increased pulse rate (tachycardia), raised blood pressure, flushed warm skin, sweats freely, has a dry mouth and widely dilated pupils. These signs indicate severe intoxication. However, in the days when amphetamines were taken in small therapeutic doses, there was usually little evidence of the drug being taken bar the fact that a person would be more cheery than usual and more talkative.

This aspect of amphetamine effects provided the clue to amphetamine-related problems. First and last the amphetamines are drugs which cause a subjective feeling of improved mood – true euphoria – and for this reason they cause states of psychological dependence. People find them universally attractive. Normally people feel euphoric when they take them. This has been demonstrated in experiments on normal subjects.

Medical uses of amphetamines   Most physicians would now agree that the therapeutic uses of amphetamines are restricted to the treatment of a rare neurological disorder – narcolepsy. In this condition the affected individual suddenly falls asleep quite inexplicably but sometimes precipitated by an unexpected stimulus such as hearing a joke. They are used in the management of over-active children (hyperkinesis), but here agreement as to their use is less definite. Finally, they may be given to patients suffering from epilepsy who are made over-sleepy by the anti-epileptic drugs they are taking.

In the past the amphetamines were used in the treatment of obesity because of their ability to affect appetite. Unhappily this effect lasted only a few weeks and the bad effects of the medication outweigh the apparent good. They were also used in the treatment of mildly depressive states – before the advent of anti-depressant drugs. Even then it was apparent that their uses were on the whole limited, because the patient would experience a worsening of the depression when the amphetamine effect wore off and tended to need a larger dosage.

In general, medical policy in the cases of persons regularly taking amphetamines for depressive states was to cut down the dosage gradually.

Common preparation of the amphetamines include amphetamine sulphate, dextroamphetamine (dexedrine), Benzedrine and methyl-amphetamine (methedrine).

Perhaps the most hazardous use of amphetamine-like drugs occurred in the use of amphetamine-barbiturate mixtures in that they produce mixed states of amphetamine and barbiturate dependence.

Clinical picture of amphetamine dependence Heavy dosage of amphetamine use produces a state of excited agitated restlessness, with associated physical changes. The individual is amazingly restless and moves around quickly, talking unceasingly. The pupils are dilated, the mouth is dry and crusted with saliva. He or she runs the tip of the tongue around the inside of the lips, and the tongue and mouth can be heard sticking as the individual talks. He or she laughs and trembles for no reason. On the other hand some heavy amphetamine users develop such a degree of tolerance that their behaviour can appear, superficially at least, to be normal. People on high doses are frequently seen picking at their cuticles and finger-nails or on their face. This is probably related to the effects of

73

amphetamine drugs on central nervous transmitters.

The history given by such a person may be unreliable but it is often found that amphetamine users start around the age of twelve. Relatives, when interviewed, describe changes in behaviour over a period of weeks or months, the most striking being that the person is awake all night, usually staying out all night and returning wide-eyed and irritable in the morning. Irritability and unprovoked rage are more than common; usually a bewildered parent describes that and says how the youngster directs his or her rages at other brothers or sisters for no reason at all. Loss of appetite, mood change and general neglect occur. These are not specific pointers to abuse of amphetamines but they provide supplementary information.

Some patterns of amphetamine usage   The patterns of amphetamine usage have changed in recent years. Twenty years or so ago, the patient's history usually involved starting at the age of fourteen or fifteen, taking amphetamine pills to stay awake and feel cheery, or indeed, to overcome social embarrassment. Passive and apathetic youngsters found amphetamine a ready source of relief for their feelings of irritable self-concern. The practice is to start with four or five tablets at a time, repeating the dose a few hours later, and taking probably up to fifty tablets in a forty-eight-hour period. At the moment there is disquieting evidence that self-injection with amphetamines is on the increase.

The relationship of amphetamine usage to delinquency is, as ever, hard to unravel. In terms of increased criminality the long-term user is probably unaffected by amphetamine use as such, since such a person is most likely to have shown coexistent or antecedent delinquent behaviour before taking up amphetamines. In this sense chronic amphetamine taking can be seen as just another facet of delinquent behaviour in disturbed youngsters.

The occasional amphetamine taker, say at weekends, presents another picture. He or she shows socially unacceptable behaviour at weekends, is hung over at the beginning of the week, and his or her work record may tend to fall off because of absenteeism. Also, relationships with family and friends tend not to fare too well because of the behaviour at the weekend.

Middle-aged amphetamine users are much less frequent than was formerly the case. Years ago people who had had amphetamines prescribed for obesity or mild depressive states tended to become psychologically quite dependent on the drug but never increased the dose, continuing to take five or six tablets a day. On the other hand their psychological dependence was quite severe simply because they were unable to stop taking them. This type of usage caused a great deal of medical concern when the *British Medical Journal* described the dangers of amphetamine usage in great detail. In the same issue the use of amphetamines for the treatment of obesity was also described!

Physical complications of amphetamine usage These include the effects of intravenous drug use, weight loss, physical self-neglect and persistent picking at the cuticles and the face. High-dosage users can develop strokes caused by raised blood pressure.

Psychiatric complications of amphetamine usage In 1958 Dr Philip Connell described amphetamine psychosis. States of disturbed behaviour occur in a setting of clear consciousness and the person becomes excited, hallucinated (hears voices, sees visions) and develops ideas of persecution (paranoid delusions). They are sometimes misdiagnosed as suffering from a schizophrenic disorder since the clinical features of amphetamine-induced psychosis are indistinguishable from a true schizophrenic disorder. The symptoms tend to settle when the person stops taking amphetamines, and there is now quite definite evidence that high-dosage, chronic amphetamine takers can develop a chronic psychosis indistinguishable from schizophrenic disorders.

Anti-social behaviour People who take amphetamines quite easily become paranoid and violent. Such violent acts are compounded if the person concerned has a badly controlled previous potential for violent behaviour.

The psychiatric hazards of amphetamine usage outweigh totally their potential medical uses, and for this reason they are now subject to strict control. The medical uses of amphetamines are now limited to the management of hyperkinetic children and narcolepsy, and rarely for over-sedated patients with epilepsy.

Cocaine

Cocaine is a powerful central nervous stimulant extracted from the leaves of the coca plant, *Erythroxylon cocoa*, which has grown wild and is cultivated quite widely in Bolivia, Peru and Colombia, where it probably forms the mainstay of the region's economy.

For more than two thousand years the coca leaf has been known to possess stimulant properties, and was widely taken by the natives of those regions who chewed it in quantities of about 2 oz a day. The stimulating effect kept them going, gave them energy and reduced their appetite. This last effect was useful since food was hard to come by but, interestingly, the harmful effects of the bad diet were to some extent offset by the fact that the coca leaf contains vitamins and some protein. Before the Spanish invasion of South America the use was to a large extent the prerogative of the upper classes, who guarded it in a rather jealous fashion. However, in the fifteenth century large areas were allocated to the cultivation of coca and it tended to be used as a form of stimulation to be given to labourers and other workers.

When the Spaniards invaded South America they tried at first to suppress its use as they felt that it contravened Christian morality. But later when they discovered that it was an aid to increased work output for the labouring classes they not only encouraged its use but the Church had its own plantations and sold and distributed coca leaves to the populace.

Cocaine was isolated from the coca leaves in the nineteenth century in Germany, where it was given its name, and in the 1880s neurologists and other physicians felt that it would be of great value in the treatment of mental disorder. Sigmund Freud himself used it and proclaimed its usefulness. He caused quite a scandal by offering it to a friend of his, a doctor who was a morphine addict, for the treatment of morphine addiction and succeeded in converting him into a cocaine addict!

Medical interest in the drug faded, however, with the realization that the stimulant effects were short lived and that the drug could cause undesirable side-effects on the heart, including sudden death. The drug was used only by relatively small groups of people right into the twentieth century.

On the other hand coca extract had a more widespread usage: first, in a variety of champagne, marketed throughout Europe and in the USA, where coca was added to the wine. Advertisements for this wine can be seen in copies of the *Illustrated London News* from 1884, and it enjoyed a wide vogue. In the early part of the century the original Coca-Cola contained coca extract but the practice was later discontinued – this popular beverage no longer contains it.

The medical uses of cocaine relate to its action as a local anaesthetic, where it has been widely used particularly in eye and oral surgery, although nowadays it is to some extent supplanted by a wider range of local anaesthetics.

Cocaine used by addicts in this country enjoyed a vogue in the 1920s among the 'bright young things'. There had been a mythical expansion of its use during the First World War – soldiers were thought to be obtaining it from prostitutes and so it was brought under stricter legal control. In fact there was no foundation for this belief. From the 1930s onwards it was probably used in Britain by a handful of people, but with the upsurge in drug usage in the 1960s certainly more people were using it. The majority of physicians stopped prescribing it, following the introduction of the special licences to prescribe, but in any case most of the patients had switched to amphetamines when they found it difficult to get cocaine. So it remained until comparatively recently when in the USA there was an explosion of cocaine use. This has not occurred to the same extent in Britain and the rest of Europe but it certainly is a more frequently used recreational drug amongst wealthier people.

Actions The primary action of cocaine on the central nervous system is one of intense stimulation. The precise mechanism of this stimulation has been postulated but as yet not completely proved. However, one thing is certain – from the point of view of producing an addictive state cocaine is probably the most powerful drug there is. The user values the euphoria produced by the drug so highly that

77

he or she wants nothing else. Animal studies in which an animal is allowed free availability to cocaine by self-injection show that the animal will inject itself with the drug continuously until it dies from heart and lung failure.

From the point of view of human use there is no physical dependence but the psychological dependence based on the state of euphoria and elation produced is intense. This is entirely drug-related in the sense that a cocaine user does not have to have severe or moderately severe psychological problems before using the drug. Anyone who takes cocaine regularly can become addicted to it very quickly. Much more quickly than to alcohol or, for that matter, to opiates.

Patterns of use   Patterns of cocaine use have not been studied in any depth in Britain and only to some extent in the USA. Indications are that some people indulge in cocaine 'binges' but very few people are able to restrict their cocaine intake to an occasional dose. Regular use invariably leads to addiction.

Methods and varieties of use   There are three main varieties of cocaine in current use. The first is cocaine powder, the powdered crystals as derived from the plant, and this preparation is either inhaled or mixed with water and injected. The next, more potent preparation of cocaine, is known as 'free base' and is a method of making pure cocaine out of adulterated street cocaine obtainable in the USA. The cocaine is boiled in ether, which produces a free drug as the process frees it from the hydrochloride or sulphate salt in which it is usually present. This preparation is highly stimulant, producing a 'rush', and the user quickly develops tolerance and needs larger doses. Thus it is immensely addictive. However, the most powerful version of all is 'crack', which has been available in the USA only in the past few years and is undoubtedly the most addictive drug there is. There may be as many as a million or more users in the USA. It first emerged in Los Angeles in the early 1980s and it is made simply by mixing powdered cocaine with water and baking soda. This is another method of removing the impurities with which street cocaine is laden, and the end product is a white mixture which is probably 90 per cent pure cocaine, and which is then dried and made into small chips and smoked. Another way in which cocaine is taken is by intravenous injection in combination with heroin, the so-called 'speedball'.

Complications of cocaine use Literature in the early part of the century created the myth of the drug-crazed killer. There is little doubt that what people were describing was psychopathic individuals highly stimulated by cocaine who had become psychotic under its influence. With the exception of alcohol, drug use does not generally lead to violent behaviour. The relation of criminality to drug use has already been considered, but this does indicate one of the most striking complications of cocaine use. That is the development of an acute paranoid psychosis in which the individual feels persecuted, has delusions of persecution, experiences hallucinations – commonly hallucinations of insects under the skin, so-called formication. It seems possible that prolonged cocaine use can lead to a chronic altered mental state in which the person remains paranoid. Other physical complications of cocaine use include erosion of the bony septum in the nose through chronic ulceration following inhalation and this can in turn lead to the development of cancer in that area. High doses can lead to irregular heart action (arrhythmias) and very large doses can cause cardiac arrest and death. The most common examples of this happening accidentally arise when people smuggle cocaine having swallowed large quantities in condoms, which are then eroded within the stomach and intestine thus causing the absorption of a huge overdose of the drug leading to death. Other complications include strokes and high fevers (hyperpyrexia).

Hallucinogenic Drugs

LSD

LSD (lysergic acid dithylamide) was synthesized in 1938 by a research chemist called Hofmann, who was working on ergot derivatives. Later he discovered its hallucinogenic properties when, accidentally, he drank some water containing LSD. Subsequently he reported its effects. In the 1950s it enjoyed a brief vogue in the treatment of some psychiatric disorders, and certainly encouraged people to think about the possibilities of brain biochemical disturbances in schizophrenic disorders. LSD though did not itself really throw any light on this. The major explosion of the recreational use of LSD was triggered off in the USA by Timothy Leary and Alpert at Harvard. Leary became a guru of the psychedelic movement and his influence caused thousands of youngsters to use the drug recreationally, many of whom came to harm as a result. It remains a popular recreational drug but does not carry the cult significance it had in the 1960s although it is the subject of revival among young people in London. It is likely that the reaction of law enforcement agencies towards LSD was prompted by its widespread use in the 1960s, and it may be that this was an overreaction. Controlling the use of LSD by legal means is probably not very practical because it is a drug which is comparatively easy to manufacture in the home given a simple knowledge of chemistry.

Other hallucinogenics   Other commonly used hallucinogenic drugs include psilocybin, mescaline, dimethyl tryptamine (DMT), Ditran and phencyclidine (PCP). Dependence on these drugs is purely psychological, no physical dependence occurs. Psychological dependence can often lead to considerable alteration of the person's way of life, quite apart from drug-induced psychosis.

The effects of hallucinogenics

The most striking effect of hallucinogenic drugs is the production of severe perceptual disturbances including hallucinations. This is not the limit of their effects and for this reason other names have been applied to the group including psychedelic (mind altering) and psychotomimetic (able to mimic manifestations of mental illness).

The emotional changes associated with hallucinogenic drugs can be extreme and include states of ecstasy, anxiety, terror, nameless dread and depression. These are frequently followed by perceptual disorders such as hallucinosis, and also distorted perceptions in which the person has the experience of hearing a colour for instance. A feeling of cosmic revelation is frequently described, of a sense of metaphysical union with the universe, and these effects are highly valued by the person who takes the drug. It is likely that one of the consequences of such an experience is that users tend to over-value such effects, often with quite disastrous consequences to themselves and others.

Adverse reactions to hallucinogens are well documented particularly following use of LSD. These include periods of intense psychotic excitement – often schizophrenic in form – depressed mood, prolonged anxiety and persistent feelings of unreality. It is now known that prolonged LSD use can lead to permanent psychotic states; in the past this was disputed but is now well established. The activity of these drugs is influenced not only by the user's personality but also by the prevailing mood and expectations of the drug effect. This is true of all mind-altering drugs for that matter including alcohol, barbiturates, opiates and amphetamines.

Naturally occurring hallucinogens are quite well documented historically. For instance, the taking of hallucinatory mushrooms by tribes in northern Siberia and the use of the sacred mushroom by Mexicans, the latter in the setting of religious observation, are well described. It has also been suggested that the state of 'berserk' described in Nordic myths may well have been caused by intoxication by the mushroom *Amanita muscaria*, which contains the hallucinogen bufotenin. The effects of hallucinogens then are dramatic and remarkable. LSD is probably the most powerful biologically active substance known. The perceptual changes extend beyond mere hallucinosis to a wide spectrum of bizarre changes in the quality of perception with intensification and distortion of images and a considerable preoccupation with the nature of the perceptual experience. Altered feelings of reality and of the self and of the environment are common and the person's thinking becomes altered. Thought processes become more diffuse and have a dreamlike quality.

Treatment

Since hallucinogenics are largely recreational the question of treatment programmes rarely arises. In practice probably the main occasions when people present in accident and emergency departments in states of excitement for treatment are following either a 'bad trip' or an LSD-induced psychosis. Experienced LSD users can usually manage to talk down someone who is experiencing a bad trip, in which they are usually extremely afraid, even terrified, and it is possible to give them maximum reassurance until they remit from this state. Sometimes, however, they do present to hospitals where their stay is usually brief and their calmness is induced by the judicious use of tranquillizers.

The management of an LSD-induced psychosis often requires hospital admission where antipsychotic medications are given until such time as the person regains his or her hold on reality and is no longer troubled by hallucinosis, feelings of persecution etc.

Classification

A convenient classification of hallucinogenic drugs includes the following.

The tryptamine group This contains substances which are straightforward derivatives of tryptamine and substances which contain the tryptamine nucleus in a ring complex structure. Simple tryptamine derivatives include dimethyl tryptamine and diethyl tryptamine, serotonin (a central nervous transmitter), bufotenin and psilocybin (the active principle of the sacred Mexican mushroom). Other hallucinogens with a basic tryptamine nucleus include LSD, harmine (used by South American Indians) and ibogaine, the active principal of the plant *Tabernathe iboge*, used in western central Africa.

Phenyl ethylamine group These are all related to what are known as the catecholamines of which the best known is mescaline, the active principal of peyote derived from the leaves of the cactus *Lophophora williamsi*. This is used in tribal and religious ceremonies in South America. Other substances in this group include TMP (trimethoxyamphetamine) and MDA (methylene dioxyamphetamine).

Mixed group The third group is a mixed one. It includes ditran, which can cause total loss of contact with the environment;

tetrahydrocannabinol, the active principle of cannabis; and phen-cyclidine (sernyl or PCP), which can cause loss of skin sensation, disturbances of the body image and states of confusion.

General comments on hallucinogenic drugs

Of all the hallucinogens LSD is the most widely known, although PCP has become a very popular street drug in the USA, though not to that extent in Britain and other Western countries. Some years ago LSD was used in psychiatric treatment and research but there was little good evidence to support its continued use. At one time it was claimed to be useful in the treatment of alcoholism but this proved not to be the case. Research interest in the hallucinogenic drugs relates mainly to the psychotic states that they can cause, often referred to as 'model psychosis'. It was thought that the investigation of 'model psychosis' might throw some light on the causes of psychoses such as schizophrenic disorders, but there is no clear evidence linking the action of hallucinogens to these causes.

It is a fact that while the hallucinogens do cause psychotic states the mechanism is not understood despite the tantalizing similarities between drug-induced psychosis and others.

The casual recreational use of hallucinogens has found fairly wide favour and seems to vary in popularity with the passage of time in much the same way that other drugs usage does. Informed opinion rightly deplores the recreational use of hallucinogenic drugs as being yet another example of the use of drugs for hedonic purposes in those situations where the illusory gains of spurious insight proffered by the drug are offset by the hazards of adverse reactions which are unpredictable in onset and duration, and often tragic in outcome.

Volatile Solvent Abuse

There are many substances which can be inhaled and are used for getting 'high'. Although it is customary to refer to these as volatile solvents, the list is actually more diverse than this although cleaning materials are probably the most prominent. In addition to these the fumes from various types of domestic glue are used as well as nail varnish, aerosols and fuels including lighter fuel and gasoline.

Fashions seem to change, at one time certain varieties of suede cleaner were popular.

In addition to this, anaesthetic gases have been frequently abused by nurses and doctors working in operating rooms. It seems likely that this practice is not as common as it was once, now that the dangers have been realized. In general, however, the most common users of solvents are young adolescent males. Usage is extremely rare in girls. In Britain it is not a nationwide problem but is found in pockets in various parts of the country.

It seems clear that the two main reasons for people using these substances are a desire to get high and pressure from their peers. Solvents are cheap, easy to obtain despite tightening of the restrictions surrounding their sale, easy to carry around and simple to administer.

Solvent inhalers can usually be picked out by a general deterioration in behaviour and appearance – something which applies to all varieties of substance abuse – but there are other obvious signs for parents. Inhalers' breath will smell of the gas, they frequently have an irritating persistent cough and they have sores round the mouth and nose after frequent inhalation. They also often tend to become careless and leave signs of their paraphernalia lying around at home.

The general effects of the substances can be summarized as a feeling of relaxation and euphoria, but if too large a dose is taken states of mental confusion will occur. The person hallucinates and displays agitated, sometimes violent behaviour under the direct influence of the drug. The main serious effect arises from over-dosage, where severe states of coma can develop even leading to death, though this is rare. Long-term effects can involve permanent liver damage and severe depression of bone marrow activity, which may be irreversible.

Tranquillizer Dependence

The tranquillizers are one of the four main groups of psychoactive drugs which have medical uses. The others are, first, the anti-depressant drugs, of which there are four main varieties. All are useful in the treatment of moderate to severe depressive states and have no abuse potential. The next group is the neuroleptic drugs. These have been in use since the early 1950s and have grown from one original medication – chlorpromazine – to a wide range of similar medications and others. Again these have absolutely no abuse potential at all, their place in the treatment of severe psychotic disorders such as schizophrenia is established and their side effects well recognized. The final group comprises lithium, which is a most valuable medication in the treatment of manic depressive disorders. Again it has no abuse potential.

Benzodiazepine tranquillizers first came into use in the late 1950s. Chlordiazepoxide (Librium) was the first, and there have since been many others, the most widely known and used probably being diazepam (Valium). Others include lorazepam (Ativan) and oxazepam (Serenid). Tranquillizers have generally been used in the relief of anxiety symptoms. Anxiety is a common disorder, is often chronic and can be crippling. It has psycho-physiological manifestations including accelerated heart rate (tachycardia), diarrhoea, loss of appetite, churning feelings in the stomach and a general feeling of tension and irritability.

Anxiety may sometimes be linked to specific situations and objects, in which case it is known as phobic anxiety. In other cases it is a diffuse disorder which may be acute or chronic. There is no doubt that in the early days of using tranquillizers for anxious patients they did provide considerable subjective relief of symptoms and numerous patients found immediate relief in this way. The dangers of tranquillizers producing dependence were first noticed in the late 1960s in Britain, when Professor Lader and colleagues at the Institute of Psychiatry in London described a small number of people who quite clearly had become dependent on tranquillizers after taking them in substantial doses for periods of a few years or more.

With the passage of time more cases were uncovered. It is easy to blame the medical profession for continuing to prescribe medications uncritically to people for periods of, say, nineteen years. To the objective observer this must seem ridiculous, but it did in fact happen. On the other hand it should be pointed out that the

85

pharmacokinetics of benzodiazepine tranquillizers were poorly understood in the early days for the simple reason that the science of pharmacokinetics, the rate at which drugs act and disperse in the body, was still very much in its infancy. The real problem with the use of the tranquillizers is that many of them, e.g. diazepam and lorazepam, have quite long half-lives. Not only that but a pharmacological 'dirty trick' is played in that tranquillizers have what is known as a biphasic half-life. At first the half-life, i.e. the time taken for the drug's potency to be reduced by half, will be, say, twenty-nine hours, but thereafter the half-life increases to about 140 hours. This means that a person is excreting only small quantities of the drug since it is tending to accumulate in the body. Undoubtedly this factor contributes to the dependence that occurs. It should also be emphasized that this is again an innocent therapeutic dependence, occurring in people who are not taking the drugs for the purpose of pleasure but purely for the relief of symptoms. They find that they develop withdrawal symptoms when they discontinue taking the medication. At first these symptoms were thought merely to be a return of the anxiety symptoms from which the patient had been suffering before taking the medication but it soon became apparent that this was not the case. Other symptoms occurred such as terrifying hallucinatory states and, where large doses of the medication had been taken, withdrawal epileptic seizures (exactly the same as in withdrawal from barbiturates).

The benzodiazepines have found some street use, mainly in heroin addicts staving off withdrawal symptoms but in general the vast majority of people involved in dependence are the innocent victims of 'treatment'.

The management of this pathetic disorder consists of very slow reduction of doses over a period of months. Many patients also find great help and assistance from support groups of fellow former tranquillizer users where they experience the same sort of support and help that is provided by organizations such as Alcoholics Anonymous.

The remedy is simple: doctors should be discouraged from prescribing tranquillizers in anything but minimal dosage for a minimal period of time never in excess of two or three weeks.

People who have anxiety symptoms of a physical sort can also get very good relief from the use of beta-blocker medications since they have no abuse potential.

Cannabis

Cannabis (marijuana, hashish, pot, ganja, etc.) is obtained from the flowering tips and leaves of *Cannabis sativa* (Indian hemp) plant which grows wild all over the world although mainly in warmer climates. It was formerly supposed that it could not be cultivated in the temperate climate of northern Europe but this is not so. The resin from the plant or the dried leaves can be used as source material as well as the dried plant. The active chemical principles of cannabis are members of the tetrahydrocannabinols. Dependence on cannabis is characterized by psychological dependence but no physical dependence occurs. The effects of cannabis include an accelerated heart rate (tachycardia) raised blood pressure, blood-shot eyes, pallor, faintness and often headache and nausea. In addition to this, recent evidence indicates that cannabis smoking produces obstructive lung disease since the smoke is extremely irritant. The cannabis smoker who is usually a cigarette smoker therefore has a further health hazard as far as heart and lung functions are concerned.

In general the cannabis-user looks for the desired effects of a carefree feeling, being talkative and feeling mildly hilarious. Unfortunately, first-time users of cannabis experience panic reactions so that all is not quite as smooth as the cannabis devotee would have one believe. Acute reactions to cannabis have been described and these include feelings of unreality, disorganized thinking and schizophrenia-like psychotic reactions.

For some time there has been controversy whether these are direct cannabis effects or reactions triggered in unstable people. Recent evidence indicates, however, that cannabis can trigger quite serious psychotic reactions. When one bears in mind that the cannabis user may also be using other hallucinogenic drugs, it cannot lightly be dismissed as a harmless recreational drug. There is no reason to suppose that cannabis smoking *per se* leads to opiate

87

usage; numerous studies have revealed that it does not. However, there is evidence linking cannabis usage to progression to the use of more powerful hallucinogenic drugs. Also, many heavy cannabis users report increased alcohol consumption.

Permanent long-term effects of cannabis have not clearly been demonstrated but there is evidence to suggest that heavy short-term use can lead people into states of disorganized inertia: what is known in the USA as the 'amotivational syndrome'. One quite definite thing about cannabis is that it is not a drug which triggers violent behaviour, in the way that alcohol does. It seems to have been given a good name and a bad name in an equally uninformed fashion.

The general feeling in regard to the question of legalizing cannabis is that usage should be decriminalized and possession should not be regarded as a particularly serious offence. The whole question of the legal controls of drug usage is considered in general terms elsewhere in this book.

The health hazards of cannabis

Of all the illicit drugs presently available, cannabis is by far the most widely used. It is known, for instance, that by 1979 more than 50 million Americans had tried it on at least one occasion. In 1981, 7 per cent of high school, senior class pupils claimed to use it daily and 46 per cent said they had used it at least once during the preceding twelve months; this level of use is probably equalled in other Western countries. Although there have been many proclamations about the supposed ill-effects of cannabis this question is far from clear. It gained a bad reputation in the USA in the 1920s purely on the basis of some rather ill-informed comments made by various public figures who were entirely ignorant of the effects of the drug. And so the myths that marijuana causes people to be drug crazed were started. In fact there is no evidence at all that links marijuana with violent behaviour of any sort, quite the reverse.

Nevertheless, the supposed ill-effects of cannabis continue to be proclaimed and so there is a need for a detailed look at what the possible effects on health may be. This was provided in the USA in a report entitled *Marijuana and Health* published in 1982 by the

National Academy of Sciences. In general the report finds that while it cannot be regarded as a harmless drug neither can it be convicted of being as dangerous as had been asserted. The report is rather indecisive: the authors were clearly worried about its widespread use but were unable to provide enough hard evidence about the extent of the risk. The main findings are that it does have dose-related effects on perception, on a person's mood and in particular on mental and physical co-ordination so that it can affect the ability to drive and operate machinery, just like alcohol. It does produce some short-term memory impairment and difficulty in learning and, again depending on dosage, a person may become anxious, excited or even delirious. These short-term psychological effects are well documented.

No convincing evidence was found that prolonged use could cause permanent changes in the central nervous system or on brain function; however, some doubt is now cast on these observations by recent Swedish findings indicating that cannabis use is likely to produce schizophrenic disorders. Cannabis does produce some stress on the circulation in that the heart beats faster and the blood pressure may rise but this is unlikely to be of much importance except in the case of somebody who has raised blood pressure. As has been noted the irritant smoke can lead to obstructive lung disease.

In the past there was concern that it might produce damage to the unborn child but the evidence for this isn't impressive.

Someone once remarked that everyone seemed to be looking for all the possible bad effects of marijuana – what about the possible good effects? There is some evidence that it is useful in reducing the raised pressure within the eye in the condition of glaucoma, and undoubtedly the active principle, delta THC, is a most valuable agent in suppressing intense nausea which people experience when undergoing chemotherapy for cancer. Apart from these no other medical uses are noted.

6

Treatment and Withdrawal

Are Alcoholism and Drug Dependence Illnesses?

When human behaviour persistently offends the sensibilities of society it is necessary to find explanations. In Western society there is a general belief that people are responsible for their actions and must bear responsibility for the consequences. This rather shaky assumption may have simple results. An individual who persistently behaves contrary to the norms of society may be categorized along a 'good ... bad' baseline and his or her behaviour may then be explained in terms of his or her position along a 'goodness ... badness' continuum. Thus frequent offenders are regarded as 'very bad', in contrast to less frequent or 'once only' offenders. The 'very bad' person may be regarded as being of 'weak character' or of 'low moral fibre' and there the matter may rest. This is obviously an over-simplification which does not account for all the vagaries of human behaviour.

When society is faced with persistent offenders, whose abnormalities of conduct start early and continue throughout adult life, it tends to react by asserting that such people must be ill; their conduct can be explained only by presupposing some form of psychological illness or some fundamental flaw in their make-up. This suggestion is usually put forward because persistently abnormal conduct does not respond to conventional forms of punishment: 'If he's so bad that punishment doesn't reform him then he must be ill.'

Dictionary definitions of health and illness tend to stress the presence of one in the absence of the other, and official definitions of such terms as 'mental illness' or 'mental health' tend to be tenuous and unhelpful. Thomas Bewley has commented on the difficulty of defining terms such as drug dependence in terms of illness. It is agreed that there are semantic difficulties involved in defining drug dependence or alcoholism entirely as illnesses, yet on the other hand there is equal agreement that to regard these two varieties of human behaviour as illnesses is a humane beginning to our understanding of them.

Perhaps the north European puritan tradition contributes to our difficulty in all this. An American commentator noted that much of the rigid public attitude towards drug abuse present in the USA for many years could be traced to the puritan attitudes brought to the USA by the early settlers from the United Kingdom, who took with them less of the *laissez-faire* hedonism of Charles I and a good deal more of the puritanism of their religious leaders.

It may be thought that the discussion of these points is merely an academic quibble but such a criticism is less than fair. We must have clear ideas about the meaning of the terms we use, and while pragmatic and humane considerations may urge us to interpret drug abuse and alcoholism as forms of sickness such an interpretation may be as simplistic as regarding both as vices, based on inherent human badness.

One difficulty is that our concept of illness is vague, indeed the concept of 'mental illness' is constantly under review. At one time the 'mentally ill' received 'custodial treatment' in asylums or prisons whenever they broke the law. But with the increase in awareness of the complexities of human behaviour, behavioural scientists have tried to categorize behaviour in a more rational way so that the sick may be treated and the wicked punished. However, we need not flatter ourselves that our catagorizations are particularly expert. The decision to give a prisoner psychiatric treatment may be arbitrary, even fortuitous, and honest psychiatrists are soon made aware of their limitations when they enter prison work. At the same time hospitals find themselves confronted with serious problems in the care of offenders who are regarded as ill. Thus when we regard the offender as 'ill' this may well be a matter of convenience stemming from humanitarian principles. It may be helpful but does not provide us with a complete explanation. There are serious gaps in our knowledge and fundamental dilemmas remain unresolved. A person who consults a psychiatrist is not necessarily suffering from a psychiatric illness just because he or she has entered the psychiatrist's office. Indeed in recent years some psychiatrists have tended to cast doubts on the reliability of their own diagnoses and in some instances to question their value at all!

To return to drug dependence and alcoholism, one is perhaps on surer ground here because the people involved with these substances frequently develop physical and psychiatric complications. Drug effects can look like psychiatric disorders or they can actually trigger them. Alcohol can cause not only deterioration of a person's mode of behaviour but also permanent brain damage (dementia) as well as transient psychotic illnesses, for example delirium tremens.

Here are concrete examples of illness about which no one would disagree. It is likely that the association of alcoholism and drug use with disease arose because physicians became aware of their consequences to physical and mental health. They then reasoned that someone who became involved with these substances was more likely to be ill than not. Even if this reasoning is not one hundred per cent cogent it does reflect a humanitarian and a sensible approach to the study of human behaviour. The pragmatic approach is an important feature of medical practice today. It is not many centuries since madmen were regarded as evil and subjected to torture and punishment. Less than seven centuries ago in Scotland epileptics were buried alive.

We might summarize by saying that the concept of mental illness takes as its starting point an individual's inability to function normally or to consider the extent of the handicap from which he or she suffers. Changes in his or her behaviour may be manifested in terms of personal, physical and social implications.

At a more sophisticated level one takes into account the effects of the 'illness' on the family, especially if it destroys the relationships within the family, and if it affects the individual's performance in the world at a professional, social and interpersonal level.

Thus to regard dependence on alcohol and on drugs as a kind of disease does constitute a humane and a practical approach in our efforts to understand a complex area of human behaviour. It should be added that in general people are more inclined to regard alcoholism and drug dependence as illnesses in their own right rather than to consider them as varieties of deviant behaviour – such as stealing. Drug addicts and alcoholics are, after all, continuously damaging themselves with toxic substances and to act in this way is, to say the least, an abnormal way of carrying on. On the other hand, one has to ask whether smoking or, for that matter, excessive gambling should be regarded as an illness. To pose such questions shows the problem is complicated. A humane pragmatic approach is therefore preferable to dogmatism.

Principles of Treatment of Drug and Alcohol Abuse

Current practice in Britain favours the use of a multi-disciplinary team approach in dealing with drug or alcohol problems. This pattern of management has derived from contemporary psychiatric practice and has considerable merit. Dealing with substance abusers on a one-to-one basis is possible and should not be pushed aside but the multi-disciplinary team approach has the great merit of sharing the load and bringing differing therapeutic skills to bear upon the patient.

The team consists of a psychiatrist, a psychologist, social workers and ideally a number of community psychiatric nurses. Psychiatry has traditionally been associated with the management of drug dependence and alcoholism. There is good sense in this since these are behavioural problems of the sort that psychiatrists might be expected to deal with. Unhappily the poor results of treatment and the bad reputation of drug users as patients have deterred many psychiatrists from involvement with this sort of work.

It should be recognized that the attitudes and feelings of the members of the team towards the patients are of paramount importance. The professionals involved need to display their acceptance of the patients for what they are, to show cautious and informed

93

optimism even in the face of what may seem intractable problems, and above all to possess a sense of realism about what it may be possible to achieve. Zealots are to be avoided at all times as members of the therapeutic team.

The individual patient or client needs to be viewed as a whole in his or her psychosocial context. At the same time the medical end of the team will need to be aware of the pharmacological effects and complications of the use of the particular substance involved. It is really no use dismissing substance abuse as 'a social problem' and leaving it at that. The pharmacological aspects are always bad – after all, they are the cause of the disturbance.

The team will then have to decide about possible short- and long-term goals for the particular person. Obviously the most desirable primary goal is that the patient should be drug free and remain so. As we have seen this is not an easily obtainable one-off goal, and it must be realized that it is the drugs or the alcohol that may cause most of the person's psychological problems and repeated treatment failures.

It is all too easy to say 'we cannot treat this person's disorder until we find out the underlying disability and problem'. This is a naïve and simplistic way of looking at things, which attracts by its very simplicity. Only over a period of time can psychiatrists discover whether the patient has deep-seated personality problems or not, and whether the drugs or the alcohol are causing further problems, be they psychological or physical.

The initial decision of the team will be whether the person needs to be treated as out-patient or attend a day centre or become an in-patient. In the case of alcohol abuse the first two alternatives are increasingly popular and less reliance is placed upon in-patient treatment except for detoxification. In general in-patient admission is determined by failure of out-patient treatment in either the short or long term, by the presence of severe physical or psychological complications of drug or alcohol abuse, and by the presence of a variety of drug abuse that may present a hazard to life during withdrawal, e.g. barbiturate dependence. Finally, the question of admission to hospital may be determined by the patient's real lack of resources in terms of hopeless social conditions and lack of family support or interest.

Detoxification programmes have been touched on elsewhere and after detoxification there is universal agreement that any sort of psychoactive medication is to be avoided at all costs.

Psychotherapy of a formal sort, e.g. psychoanalysis, is hardly if ever used but other psychotherapeutic approaches are quite extensively used at either an individual or group level. In determining what sort of psychotherapy may be needed, the needs of the individual patient must be identified. Does he or she require straightforward counselling or perhaps something more subtle of an interpretative sort. In general, current practice favours the former dealing with the here and now rather than looking for buried treasure in the unconscious.

The use of psychotherapy is somewhat contentious as, in therapy, the role of the doctor, psychologist, social worker and community psychiatric nurse may overlap considerably. But whoever is involved in giving psychotherapy the important simple principles are to settle reasonably attainable goals and to agree these with the patient. In a sense a contract is made and indeed many programmes offer a written contract which the patient signs. Above all, intelligent and sensible support is vital since many drug and alcohol users pass through one series of crises after another and during these they need support. If one is using some probing form of psychotherapy it is also important to try to look for elements of anxiety and depression which may be linked to drug use. They may be caused by drug use or the patient may be using drugs to relieve the symptoms.

Self-help groups such as Alcoholics Anonymous are important and may often be the prime therapeutic agency. Family support groups are another important service which can be offered to the family of the user. These have mushroomed all over Britain and many of them are outstanding in their practice.

Methadone Maintenance

In New York in the early 1960s Doctors Vincent Dole and Marie Nyswander published their findings on the use of methadone as maintenance treatment in heroin addiction. The idea of giving a maintenance drug or a substitute was a particularly hot topic in the USA at the time and remains so. This had come about because in the 1920s it had been possible for doctors to prescribe morphine for morphine addicts and these clinics, it is now known, worked very well. But the clinics and the doctors concerned were subjected to vilification and persecution by Treasury Agents. This is a matter of historical fact which no one now seriously questions. The work being carried out at these clinics was misrepresented to the public by physicians, and eventually after great harassment the clinics were closed down. However, it is now known that their results were good and people received a good standard of care.

Thereafter the influence and intimidating attitude of the authorities were such that doctors would have nothing to do with addicts and certainly no form of prescribing policy was ever adopted. But it went further than this in that doctors were intimidated by the authorities to such an extent that cancer patients in need of pain relief were unable to obtain it. To a large extent this puritanical attitude persists in the USA. Such an attitude towards the use of drugs did not exist in Britain although is now beginning to creep in.

It will therefore be understood that when the idea of maintenance medication for heroin addicts was voiced in New York in the 1960s, it had a mixed reception. The rationale of the treatment was simple and based in particular on Dr Nyswander's experience. She had been a practising psychiatrist for many years involved in trying to treat addicts and had found that no matter how intensive and well planned her attempts at psychotherapeutic intervention, they were on the whole to no avail. So she began to look for medication that could be given to heroin users in the hope that they might stop craving the drug and stop indulging in drug-seeking behaviour with the attendant delinquency.

She and Dr Dole came up with methadone as a likely medication to use on the basis that it had a long half-life, and did not produce 'highs' followed by bouts of withdrawal symptoms as does heroin, which has a short half-life. So methadone was given to long-term heroin users. The first patients treated were started on methadone in hospital and the dose was gradually built up until it could be shown that the drug produced a narcotic 'blockade'. This is to say if the person was given an injection of morphine or heroin they did not experience a 'high'. The early results were extremely encouraging, in that patients receiving a once-daily oral dose of methadone not only avoided getting 'high' but also ceased craving the drug and felt more 'straight', i.e. more stable, throughout the twenty-four-hour period. They were able to find employment and adopt a settled way of life without resorting to criminal activity.

The general feeling now is that methadone maintenance has not quite lived up to the early expectations but nevertheless it remains an important form of replacement treatment for the person who finds it impossible to get into a programme of total abstention. In practice it is a treatment that needs considerable supervision. Patients are expected to provide urine samples on a random or regular basis to ensure they are taking methadone and that they are not taking other drugs that they shouldn't. Before inducing the patient into a methadone programme it is necessary to make a careful evaluation of the patient with repeated samples which demonstrate the presence of heroin in the urine. Certain basic criteria are employed; for instance, in New York a person must have a minimum two-year history of heroin usage and be over the age of eighteen. Further guidelines used in this treatment suggest that after two years on methadone maintenance the patient should be admitted to hospital, withdrawn from the drug, and his or her condition reassessed. Unhappily, methadone maintenance has in some quarters established a bad reputation because the methadone programmes have not been as carefully supervised as they might. On the other hand it is certainly true that in the USA federal interference with methadone programmes has made many of them unworkable. For instance, no more than fifty patients may be taken on in a programme and the paperwork has been made so extensive that it has been calculated that it can take up to 150 per cent of the physician's time. This suggests that the inherent puritanism of the US authorities still pervades.

In the early days of methadone usage in Britain no such puritanical attitude existed, except towards the prescribing of heroin as a maintenance drug, a practice which has now virtually ceased – in

the author's opinion for no really valid reason. Methadone maintenance programmes now are much less influential and the tendency is towards the use of short-term methadone detoxification for
the newly diagnosed heroin addict. There is some merit in this
policy since at the present time the average heroin user is likely to
have a brief history, and to be smoking rather than injecting the
drug. For such a person short-term detoxification with methadone
is an ideal treatment method but adopting this policy in blanket
fashion seems rather hard on those addicts with a long history of
maybe twenty or more years behind them who have been managing
perfectly well on methadone. The question remains unresolved,
and the suspicion remains that emotional rather than valid scientific
reasons lie behind the U-turn on methadone. Time will show, but
in fairness it should be said that maintenance of opiates or opiate-
like drugs for the addict can often place an intolerable strain on the
doctor concerned. The constant fear is that the addict is selling
some of the medication he or she is receiving. The Americans have
avoided this by having methadone clinics where the patient attends
every day to receive a dose of methadone and drinks it in the
presence of a nurse so that there can be no diversion of the drug. In
Britain it was never possible to do this due to the way in which
clinics were set up, and economic reasons dictated that patients
should receive their supplies from retail pharmacists. This means
attending daily or every two days to collect medication, which is
then taken home. Clearly this has great potential for abuse. In
addition to this doctors in general do not like to feel that they are
colluding in a person's disordered condition, i.e. prolonging their
state of addiction, a fear that needs to be respected. Unhappily,
however, the fact is that drug users will go on taking drugs and if in
the last resort a maintenance method of treatment must be used, it
should be given a fair trial. It should be emphasized, however, that
maintenance treatment has a place only in the field of opiate
dependence. It has absolutely no place in the treatment of alcohol
or sedative dependence, or in the case of central stimulant and
cocaine dependence.

Another difficulty facing the doctor in maintenance treatment is
the demanding and importunate way in which many, though not all,

patients behave – wanting increased dosages, claiming to have lost drugs, and so on. Patients who continue in a satisfactory and co-operative manner with their treatment and give the doctor no problems are therefore likely to be the most popular. Paradoxically, the patients who appear to be 'managing' best may well be the ones most likely to be selling half the drugs they receive on prescription! Working in this type of practice is exasperating for all but the most saintly. Addicts are not an easy group of people to deal with and this can be particularly true where maintenance medication is on offer. Ideally the patients in the maintenance programme should be attending the clinic at least once a week for group or individual therapy. The object of this is to needle, persuade, cajole and generally edge the person towards the idea of abstention and adopting a drug-free way of life.

Finally, it should be said that prescribing injectable drugs for patients is in general discouraged though many feel there is some merit in the practice since it does at least ensure that the patient receives a clean sterile supply of the drug and also needles and syringes. Medical feelings were against the prescribing of needles and syringes until the recent emergence of the AIDS epidemic. Unsterile self-injection is an important route for spreading the AIDS virus, and the practice of providing sterile needles and syringes is now becoming more widespread. The most dramatic example of the consequence of not having sterile syringes available comes from Edinburgh, which had the highest incidence of the AIDS virus among self-injectors. The National Health Service clinic had been closed so that the addicts had to rely on shared needles and syringes, with the inevitable result of high incidence of AIDS and AIDS sero-positivity. The full implications of this experience have yet to be appreciated.

In the United Kingdom just as in the US, methadone maintenance as a treatment continues to provoke unnecessary controversy. A recent review of this problem in the American literature makes several telling points. The first consideration is that despite its social overtones and aspects, addiction is primarily a medical problem involving the interaction of a drug with a living person. Methadone maintenance is therefore a medical method of treatment and its prescription and management are fundamentally a medical responsibility. Unhappily, because of the social overtones of addiction the prime responsibility, in the USA to a great extent and in Britain to a lesser extent, has been taken out of the hands of the medical clinician. The reason for this is not hard to see, and is dictated by the fact that here is a medical treatment which can not only affect a person's behaviour but also bestow benefit on society by reducing delinquency and keeping a person in a steady job. This sort of consideration is taken into account particularly in the USA when allowing someone to enter such a programme. In some states the funding agencies insist that individuals cannot receive methadone unless they are attending regularly for counselling in relation to problems, social and otherwise (even if they don't have any). It is hard to see why such conditions should be imposed on someone who is receiving a medical treatment and these must be unique in the whole field of medical practice.

An analogy may be drawn between this process and that of a physician treating sexually transmitted diseases. A patient presents with gonorrhoea: the treatment consists of the administration of the appropriate antibiotic. It is as simple as that. No one would seriously suggest that people could not be admitted to a treatment programme unless they attended for sexual counselling to determine whether they had deep-seated psychosexual problems underlying their promiscuity. Indeed, to withhold antibiotics from a patient with gonorrhoea for those reasons would quite speedily lead to a black market in penicillin and other antibiotics, just as unhappily, has occurred in the USA where difficulty in entry into methadone maintenance programmes has led to a black market in methadone.

Withdrawal from Drugs and Alcohol

There are only three varieties of drug dependence which present real physical problems in management in the withdrawal state: opiate dependence, hypnosedative dependence (barbiturates and benzodiazepine tranquillizers) and alcohol dependence.

Opiate dependence and withdrawal regime

Opiate dependence withdrawal symptoms do not present a hazard to life but the subjective discomfort experienced by the patient can be extremely unpleasant and if severe may lead the person to discharge himself or herself from hospital prematurely. The main symptoms can be summarized in the addicts' jargon 'running at both ends', i.e. the patient has a runny nose, diarrhoea, nausea and vomiting. A general feeling of illness prevails, with pains in the legs and abdominal cramps.

Medication is useful in withdrawal states. The best medication is methadone, given by mouth, two or three times a day gradually reducing over a period of several days. Other medications that can be used include clonidine, a drug used in the treatment of high blood pressure, which has a place in in-patient opiate withdrawal. Finally, there is a place for the use of beta-blocking drugs such as propanolol. But whatever medications are used the general nursing care of the patient is very important. This includes the patient receiving a balanced diet with vitamins and plenty of fluids, but also general support and encouragement through the withdrawal period.

Withdrawal from hypnosedatives

Barbiturates and similar drugs produce physical dependence. The withdrawal syndrome is a hazard to life if the patient develops withdrawal fits, inhales vomit and asphyxiates. To avoid this patients are maintained in a state of barbiturate intoxication and doses are reduced slowly over a period of days, even weeks.

The patient is given the 'pentobarbitone challenge test': the patient receives 200 mg of pentobarbitone and the status is assessed after one hour. This clinical test enables the clinician to work out what dosage level of pentobarbitone should be used in withdrawal. For instance, if the patient is asleep after one hour this indicates that no withdrawal medication is needed. If the patient is drowsy with slurred speech this determines a level of dosage and so on.

Withdrawal from benzodiazepine tranquillizers is best done as an out-patient. Withdrawal may take months and is done slowly. The hazard to life from withdrawal fits is possible but not common or as severe a risk as in the case of barbiturates.

Withdrawal from alcohol

In severe alcohol dependence withdrawal fits occur. The withdrawal period is therefore covered with medication that stops fits. Two medications are favoured: chlordiazepoxide (Librium), which is given in substantial doses over a period of up to five days and gradually reduced; or chlormethiazole (Heminevrin), a powerful anti-convulsant which is given in reducing doses over a period of about five days.

Central stimulant drugs

Withdrawal from central stimulant drugs such as the amphetamines and related substances and from cocaine presents no physical hazards so these drugs can be stopped. If the patient is agitated and tense, sensible medication with benzodiazepines is appropriate for a few days. Better practice uses neuroleptics such as chlorpromazine (Largactil).

General comments on withdrawal regimes

The hazards of drug withdrawal are often overstated. Medication used judiciously plays a part but sensible nursing and general medical management are the mainstay of treatment.

Withdrawal from opiate drugs such as heroin for outpatients is often carried out because current heroin users – particularly smokers – are not severely physically dependent and can be withdrawn, taking methadone in small doses daily on a reducing programme for a period of four to six weeks.

Only when withdrawal is over do the real problems of management begin.

Rehabilitation: the Therapeutic Community

The term 'therapeutic community' was coined in the late 1940s by Dr Maxwell Jones, a psychiatrist who had been involved with the rehabilitation of members of the armed services during the Second World War. These were soldiers, sailors and airmen who had been unable to continue serving due to the behavioural problems they had developed in the face of intolerable stress – in other words, they cracked up. Hitherto the approach had been to subject the individual to rigorous bullying or to intensive individual psychotherapy. Rankers tended to receive the former, officers the latter. As it happened, the results in either instance were far from satisfactory.

Dr Jones found that by involving the patients in a climate of group therapy where each person would be expected to bear responsibility for his or her actions and be responsible to the rest of the group, a wide range of behavioural problems could be dealt with.

After the war he and his colleagues took this further, into the field of anti-social behaviour. In the early days they dealt with highly anti-social people – those who would now be called sociopaths – and found that they could achieve good results with such people while remaining in the community. From this he derived the idea that the community itself was therapeutic – hence therapeutic community.

Whatever the flaws of this concept may have been the fact remains that this idea has influenced rehabilitation of people with behavioural disorders all over the world. The person who enters such a community is asked to accept the conditions of the community. He or she must accept the notion of individual responsibility. For many such people such a notion must seem incredible since hitherto they have been told only that they have been the victims of circumstances, family influences, peer group pressure – anything except the idea that they might just bear some responsibility for the consequence of their actions.

There are many therapeutic communities and they come in many colours. Ultimately all acknowledge this stated belief. And there is good sense in this. It is possible that psychiatrists have for too long discarded the idea that an individual can be responsible for what he or she does. The therapeutic community challenged this negative assumption.

Life in a therapeutic community is abrasive. Confrontation on all sorts of issues is the rule of the day and this may lead the person concerned, if he or she is deemed to have broken the rules of the community, to a fair amount of humiliation and in some instances degradation. In this respect some of the therapeutic communities may appear to have gone too far. At the same time, people have emerged from such rehabilitative processes and been able to lead a drug- or alcohol-free life, and often claim that the hard times they may have experienced within the community have been of benefit to them.

It is easy to criticize therapeutic communities on methodological grounds in the sense that their results may never have been properly evaluated according to proper statistical criteria. But at the same time it has to be acknowledged that the people working in such difficult professional environments do their utmost to achieve good results. No one can criticize their professional integrity and commitment.

Rehabilitation

Rehabilitating the drug user and the alcohol user presents differing problems. This is mainly due to the fact that drug use is illicit and alcohol use is not, so that relapse is easier for the alcohol user.

The drug user will usually have been in an in-patient facility often followed by a period in a therapeutic community. The process of rehabilitation begins from day one. The object is to return the person to the community in a state where he or she will be able to remain immune from drug use. This is never easy since the patient will have spent the preceding few years of life with other drug users and will probably have been unemployed. A person's chances of achieving successful rehabilitation are best if employment is available. With the current high rates of unemployment the prospects for the drug user are pretty bleak. Nevertheless it is unwise to be over-pessimistic.

Put at its simplest level it could be said that rehabilitation, however achieved, is a combination of persuasion and occupation. Whether this course is backed up by a strongly religious influence, as in some rehabilitation facilities, or by a therapeutic community atmosphere probably matters very little. What counts most is the patient's ability to commit himself or herself to the project in hand. It is wrong to write people off as 'once an addict always an addict'. Often the apparently most hopeless individuals can find reserves within themselves of which they were quite unaware and it is by tapping these that the rehabilitation programme in which the person is involved will ultimately be judged. Peer group pressure from other inmates is important as is the attitude of the staff but ultimately the day comes when the person steps out of the institution into the world. Careful follow-up is essential but not always possible since the person may have come some distance to participate in the treatment and rehabilitation process.

In the case of the alcohol abuser, Alcoholics Anonymous is always extremely helpful and can provide placement in hostels for those unable to find accommodation, and thus provide some form of supportive shelter and encouragement.

The NHS, voluntary bodies and Social Services departments also provide similar facilities. Finally, in the field of rehabilitation of alcohol and drug users, the Probation Service, as ever, provides much pragmatic help in its customary underpaid and undervalued role.

7

Summing Up

Having looked at the problems of substance abuse over many years one remains in a state of doubtful perplexity. Uncertainty and factionalism prevail. The fact that human beings do tend to intoxicate themselves for a variety of reasons is worth repeating, in the hope that we might be honest enough to admit that none of us knows quite why they need to do this. One cannot legislate against human folly.

There are a number of points that can be made at the end of it all. Xenophobia is an important feature in our views of the problems of drug addiction. When the Chinese migrant workers came to the West Coast of the USA to build the railroads they brought their opium habits with them and nobody cared at all. People became angry only when local workers feared that the Chinese workers would compete in the labour market. They were then denounced as opium smokers. In the same way the novels of Sax Rohmer concerning the activities of Dr Fu Manchu depicted this Chinese doctor as a sinister drug user. There is little doubt that this type of xenophobia contributed quite significantly to the negative image of the opium smoker.

Black Americans have been denigrated in much the same way. It happens that a significant majority of drug users in the USA are Blacks. This applies to all drugs, whether heroin, cocaine or cannabis, and has led to the notion of a 'Black drug menace'. Something that has been echoed by a leading politician in Britain who has spoken of the country being 'rather swamped by an alien culture' and that Britain was 'up against a determined effort to flood the country with hard drugs to corrupt our youth – to undermine the stability of our country'. This is of course pure nonsense tinged with racism.

Another unhelpful myth is the notion of 'the war on drugs'. The USA and other countries have spent vast sums of money in these so-called 'wars' and at the same time have failed to see the whole exercise as more or less a waste of time and money. Investigation into the causes and control of addiction, and the proper care and rehabilitation of drug abusers would be much more useful.

The legal restriction of drugs such as heroin and cocaine needs to be constantly reviewed in terms of its effectiveness in curbing addiction. However, no sensible person would recommend setting up shops that sold such drugs. Cocaine particularly needs rational control. In any event, making such drugs freely available is bound to be self-defeating: the already highly organized criminal drug dealers would see to it that such outlets were soon put out of business. One has only to consider the example of methadone maintenance clinics in the USA, where medical directors have been threatened by the drug dealers afraid of losing lucrative trade.

Heroin is another matter. No one would suggest free availability but consideration should be given to making it more available upon prescription by licensed doctors in a sensible and rational fashion, for reasons given in this book. This could be done; it *was* done in Britain, in the past when the number of heroin addicts was small. Today it would be much less easy to administer but at the same time the case for reasonable availability of prescribed heroin remains something that should be reconsidered. The tendency has been to do away with the practice. In the author's view this is an exercise in throwing out the baby with the bathwater.

The control of intoxicating substances remains a political issue. As such debate over the best ways to proceed tends to generate more heat than light. A good deal of hypocrisy is involved, particularly in our attitudes towards the promotion of alcohol and tobacco and our condemnation of illicit substances. Those who suffer are the drug users who, because of society's attitudes, are deprived of the care and support they so desperately need.

Further Reading

Berridge, V., *Opium and the People*, Yale University Press, New Haven, 1987.

Fazey, C., *The Aetiology of Psychoactive Substance Abuse*, UNESCO, Paris, 1976.

Glatt, M. M., *Alcohol, our Favourite Drug*, Royal College of Psychiatrists, London, 1983.

Kessel, W. and Walton, H., *Alcoholism*, Penguin, London, 1979.

Maier, H. W., *Cocainism*, Addiction Research Foundation, Toronto, 1987.

Stewart, T., *The Heroin Users*, Pandora, London, 1987.

Trebach, A. S., *The Great Drug War*, Harvard University Press, Massachusetts, 1986.

Zinberg, N. E., *Drugs, Set and Setting*, Yale University Press, New Haven, 1984.

Index

Tabernathe iboge, 82
tea, 42
temazepam, 41
Temperance Movement, 56
Tenuate, 40
tetrahydrocannabinol, 83, 87
theft, 46–7
theories of drug abuse, 24–8
therapeutic communities, 102–4
thiopentone, 69
TMP, *see* trimethoxyamphetamine, 82
tobacco, *see* smoking
tolerance, 17, 30
trafficking, 37, 39, 41, 50
tranquillizers:
    abuse of, 14, 23
    alcohol and, 19
    dependence, 84–7
    legislation, 37, 41
    opium, 46
treatment of drug and alcohol abuse,
    93–5
triazolam, 41
trimethoxyamphetamine (TMP), 82
tryptamine, 82

Ulster, 18–19
United Kingdom:
    AIDS, 47–9
    alcohol, 55
    delinquency, 43–7
    General Health Questionnaire, 67–8
    history of drug abuse, 5, 11–14
    methadone programmes, 97–100,
        107

Single Convention, 50
    xenophobia, 106–7
United Nations, 50
United States of America:
    AIDS, 47–8
    alcohol, 55
    attitude to drug abuse, 6, 91, 96
    attitude to narcotics, 12, 96
    cannabis, 7, 13, 88–9
    Chinese immigrants, 106
    delinquency, 43, 46
    gender of abusers, 5
    General Health Questionnaire, 67–8
    methadone programmes, 95–7,
        99–100
    National Cancer Institute, 63
    Prohibition, 18, 22, 34, 51
    war on drugs, 50, 107

Valium, 40, 85
Vatuk, S.J., 9n.
Vatuk, V.P., 9n.

West Indians, 13
Winick, Charles, 25
withdrawal regimes, 100–2
withdrawal symptoms:
    alcohol, 53–4, 102
    barbiturate, 70
    benzodiazepine, 86
    criterion for dependence, 16–17
    hypnosedative, 101
    opiate, 101
    types of, 30–1
women, 27, 56